THINGS TO MAKE FOR CHILDREN
·TOYS·TOGS
·PARTY FUN
A Sunset Book

By the editorial staffs of
Sunset Books & Sunset Magazine

LANE BOOKS · MENLO PARK, CALIFORNIA

ABOUT THIS BOOK

The surest way in the world to make a child's eyes light up is to give him a present. And if *you*—his mother or father or grandma or grandpa or aunt or uncle—happen to have made the gift yourself, it will hold a very special place in the child's heart and your own as well.

On the pages that follow you will find dozens of ideas for things to make for children, as well as many suggestions for birthday parties and other occasions. Parents of children between 5 and 12 years of age will find this book especially useful, although there are some ideas aimed at pleasing a very small toddler and some with junior teen-age appeal. On many of the projects, parents and children can work together. Den mothers, teachers, and scout troop leaders also will find new fun projects.

Most of the examples in the book have appeared in the pages of *Sunset Magazine*. Many are first-hand contributions from readers. In selecting and organizing material the editors of *Sunset Books* were assisted by Marian May, a former *Sunset* staff member who originated some of the ideas for her own two youngsters. Because many parents have had only average craft experience, most selections were chosen for their simplicity.

A companion *Sunset* book, *Children's Rooms and Play Yards,* contains hundreds of ideas for children's bedrooms, playrooms, furniture, storage, and play equipment.

PHOTOGRAPHERS

Doris Aller: 7, 73, 77. Jerry Anson: 76 (lower). William Aplin: 63 (lower right), 93. Ernest Braun: 33, 42 (upper right), 59, 65, 72 (upper left), 85 (lower right), 86, 95. Carroll C. Calkins: 62 (middle right), 76 (upper photos). Frances Callahan: 10 (middle right). Clyde Childress: 11 (upper right, middle right, lower right), 16, 22, 23, 29 (middle right), 32, 36, 37, 48 (upper left, lower left), 50, 58. Frank R. Chow: 55 (lower left). Glenn M. Christiansen: 39, 40, 41, 53 (upper right), 75 (lower left, lower middle). Robert Cox: 28 (lower left, upper right, lower right), 29 (upper right), 30, 34 (middle left, lower left, lower right), 35 (lower left, lower right), 53 (lower right), 54, 56, 57 (upper left, lower left, lower right), 67 (upper right), 68, 80, 87, 88, 89. Virginia Davidson: 51 (upper photos). Jeanette Grossman: 47 (lower left). Russell Illig: 72 (upper right, lower right). Esther Litton: 21. Grace M. Miller: 47 (lower left). Charles R. Pearson: 66 (lower left). Tom Riley: 61. Wilma C. Simpson: 62 (lower left). Blair Stapp: 4, 10 (lower), 20, 29 (lower right), 38, 44, 45, 46, 49 (upper left), 51 (lower right), 52, 62, (upper left), 63 (upper left), 66 (upper left), 75 (upper right, lower right), 81, 83, 85 (upper right), 90, 91, 92. Darrow M. Watt: 12, 13, 14, 17, 18, 26, 27, 28 (upper left), 31, 34 (upper left), 35 (upper right), 42 (lower right), 48 (lower right), 49 (upper right, lower right), 53 (lower left), 55 (upper right), 57 (upper right), 70, 71, 78, 79, 82, 84, 94. R. Wenkam: 10 (middle left), 75 (upper left). Mason Weymouth: 19, 24, 67 (lower right). R. Widmann: 69. Alex Williams: 10 (upper), 60. Cover by Chet Martin.

Fourteenth Printing August 1972

ALL RIGHTS RESERVED THROUGHOUT THE WORLD. THIS BOOK, OR PARTS THEREOF, MAY NOT BE REPRODUCED IN ANY FORM WITHOUT PERMISSION OF PUBLISHERS. FIRST EDITION. COPYRIGHT © 1961 BY LANE MAGAZINE & BOOK COMPANY, MENLO PARK, CALIFORNIA. LIBRARY OF CONGRESS NO. 61-8397. LITHO IN U. S. TITLE NO. 470.

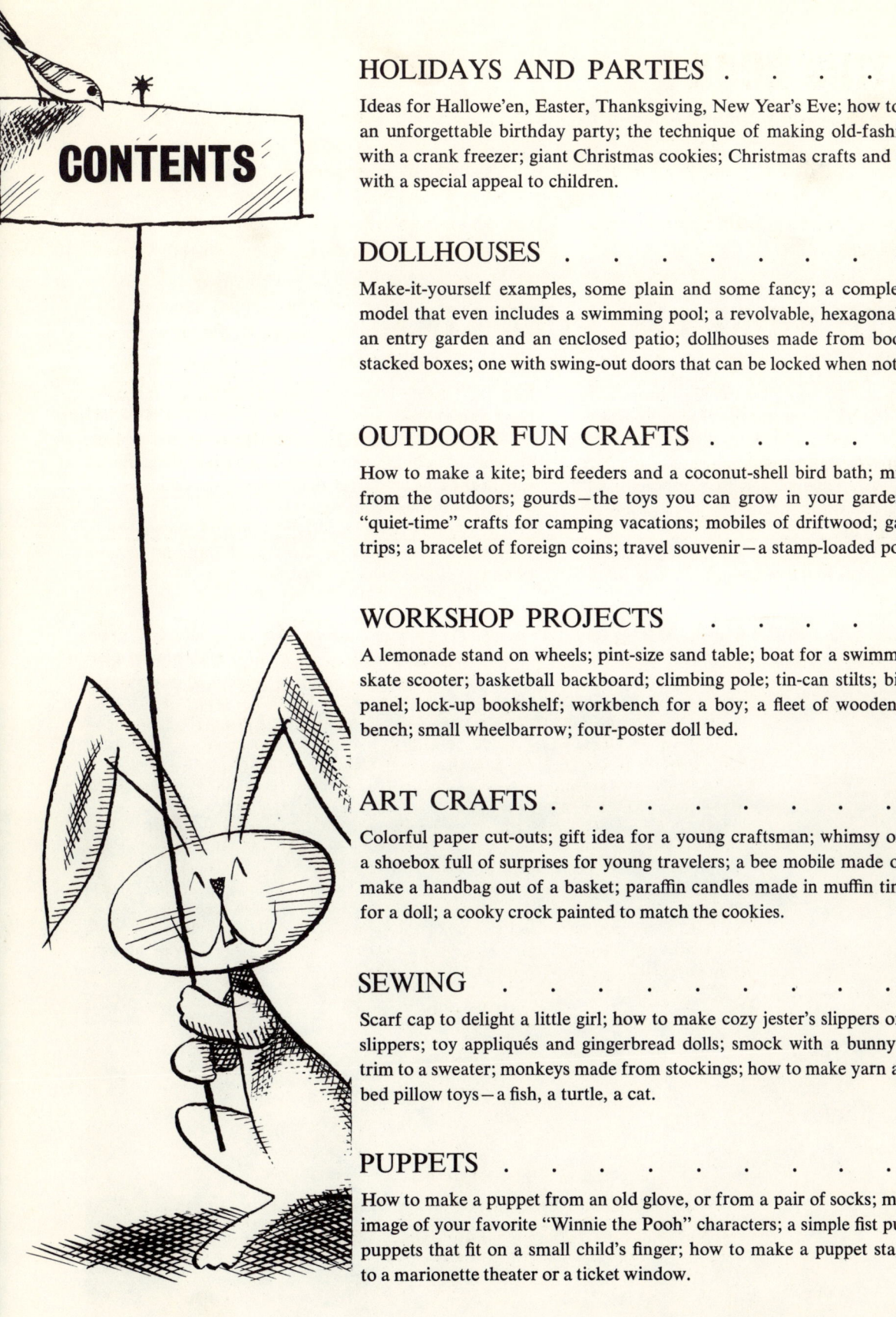

CONTENTS

HOLIDAYS AND PARTIES 4
Ideas for Hallowe'en, Easter, Thanksgiving, New Year's Eve; how to give your child an unforgettable birthday party; the technique of making old-fashioned ice cream with a crank freezer; giant Christmas cookies; Christmas crafts and decorating ideas with a special appeal to children.

DOLLHOUSES 36
Make-it-yourself examples, some plain and some fancy; a completely landscaped model that even includes a swimming pool; a revolvable, hexagonal dollhouse with an entry garden and an enclosed patio; dollhouses made from bookcases or from stacked boxes; one with swing-out doors that can be locked when not in use.

OUTDOOR FUN CRAFTS 44
How to make a kite; bird feeders and a coconut-shell bird bath; miniature gardens from the outdoors; gourds—the toys you can grow in your garden; sand casting; "quiet-time" crafts for camping vacations; mobiles of driftwood; games to take on trips; a bracelet of foreign coins; travel souvenir—a stamp-loaded postcard.

WORKSHOP PROJECTS 58
A lemonade stand on wheels; pint-size sand table; boat for a swimming pool; roller-skate scooter; basketball backboard; climbing pole; tin-can stilts; bike racks; secret panel; lock-up bookshelf; workbench for a boy; a fleet of wooden ships; tot-sized bench; small wheelbarrow; four-poster doll bed.

ART CRAFTS 70
Colorful paper cut-outs; gift idea for a young craftsman; whimsy on a child's wall; a shoebox full of surprises for young travelers; a bee mobile made of paper; how to make a handbag out of a basket; paraffin candles made in muffin tins; basket cradle for a doll; a cooky crock painted to match the cookies.

SEWING 78
Scarf cap to delight a little girl; how to make cozy jester's slippers or cool Hawaiian slippers; toy appliqués and gingerbread dolls; smock with a bunny pocket; adding trim to a sweater; monkeys made from stockings; how to make yarn animals; take-to-bed pillow toys—a fish, a turtle, a cat.

PUPPETS 90
How to make a puppet from an old glove, or from a pair of socks; marionettes in the image of your favorite "Winnie the Pooh" characters; a simple fist puppet; miniature puppets that fit on a small child's finger; how to make a puppet stage that converts to a marionette theater or a ticket window.

HOLIDAYS & PARTIES

FUN WITH KNIFE AND PUMPKIN

One of the simplest and most entertaining projects for parents and children to do together is to make a jack-o'-lantern. For best (and safest) results, the knife work should be entrusted to Dad, while Mom gathers the decorating materials. The children can then proceed—with some adult supervision—to attach the features and the trim, using glue or pins.

To carve a pumpkin, first cut off the top. Slant the knife into the pumpkin so the inside of the top is *smaller* than the outside (this keeps top from falling through). Next, remove seeds.

You get a better effect with the features if you use the opposite cutting technique: Slant the knife so the inside of the cuts are *larger* than the outside, then push the cut pieces through and remove.

In addition to the decorating materials shown below, you can use corn candy, feathers, beads, buttons, sequins, rick-rack, braid, or crepe paper.

Hallowe'en heads in a weird and wonderful variety. Pumpkins wear wigs of green onion tops, carrot tops, endive. Features of carrots, pea pods, radishes, green onions, and apple wedges are applied with pins or glue.

Long before learning how to read a calendar, a child develops a knack for "dividing up" the early years with holiday landmarks. He awaits these occasions with anxiety, and at times it seems as though the next celebration will *never* come. In this chapter are dozens of ideas for parents who wish to create some truly memorable holiday happiness and party fun.

- HALLOWE'EN: Pumpkins, costumes...
- EASTER: Fancy bunnies, lively egg hunts.
- THANKSGIVING: Ideas for decorating the children's table.
- NEW YEAR'S EVE: An early evening party.
- BIRTHDAYS: A potpourri of party ideas.
- CHRISTMAS: Giant cookies, homemade gifts, craft ideas, a cloud of angels...

HOW TO GROW A HALLOWE'EN PUMPKIN BIG ENOUGH TO PUT LITTLE BROTHER IN

Who's for growing Hallowe'en pumpkins two, three, or four times as big as the ones they sell in the stores in October? We know many a third to sixth grader who would be delighted at the opportunity — given the go-ahead, the seeds (15 cents), the space (10 by 10 feet in the sun), and some good advice.

CHOICE OF VARIETIES

The first step in growing big pumpkins is to choose a naturally big variety. Don't buy those called Small Sugar, Sugar, or New England Pie unless you want lots of little pumpkins, 6 to 8 inches across.

The varieties you can grow as big as 30 to 40 inches in diameter are called Connecticut Field and Jack O'Lantern.

PLANTING AND CARE

Plant pumpkin seeds after danger of frost is past in the spring. This is usually about mid-May. If a cold night comes along after the seeds have sprouted, cover the young plants at sundown with a large can or box; but remove it in the morning. Pumpkin plants must have sunlight to manufacture food for growth.

Choose a sunny location for pumpkin vines. The plants grow large, so figure that a single planting will cover an area 8 to 12 feet in diameter.

To produce big pumpkins, the vines need fertilizer as they grow. After soil is cultivated, scoop out a hole 4 inches deep, right under where you will plant the seeds. Put a shovelful of manure in the hole and cover it with enough soil to make the ground level again.

Plant 6 to 8 seeds, 1 inch deep, within a circle 6 inches in diameter. If you want more than one set of vines, plant hills or clusters 8 feet apart. Water the seeds after planting.

When the plants are 4 to 6 inches high, cut off the tops of all but two of the best plants in the circle.

Water the plants whenever you see signs of the slightest wilting in the leaves, but don't wet the foliage if you can help it. Water on leaves encourages disease.

When you see small pumpkins 2 to 3 inches in diameter, remove all but 3 or 4 fruits on each vine. Or, for extra large pumpkins, remove all but one pumpkin from each vine. Remove fruits toward ends of vines; save those near the main stem. Keep removing later flowers.

As a rule, pests are not very troublesome on pumpkin plants. If you do notice insects eating the leaves, spray with a multi-purpose insecticide. If you notice mildew on the leaves, dust with sulfur every 10 days.

HARVESTING THE PUMPKINS

You can pick the pumpkins after they get hard, or leave them on the vines until just before Hallowe'en if it doesn't rain. If it begins to storm, harvest the pumpkins and put them in a cool (55° to 60°) spot. Leave stems attached to the pumpkins when you cut them.

SOME EXTRA TRICKS WITH PUMPKINS

- *Making odd-shaped pumpkins.* Do you want a goblin pumpkin with a body as well as a head? Try this: When the young, growing pumpkin is about the size of a softball, tie a wide belt or a strong piece of cloth securely around the midsection of the fruit. This will restrict expansion of the center while the ends continue to grow, making a dumbbell shape. Set the pumpkin on end when it is mature and you will have a Jack O'Lantern with head and body.

- *Writing on the pumpkin.* Write your name, initials, or any message or design you choose on the young pumpkin when it is about twice the size of a softball and while the skin is still tender. Use a blunt pencil, breaking the skin lightly. The initials will callus over, grow with the pumpkin and — later — will contrast sharply with the bright yellow skin.

- *Another way to force extra growth.* This is a trick that 4-H Club members and others have used to grow extra-large exhibition pumpkins. When the pumpkin is half-mature (about 10 inches in diameter), cut a slit in the stem (between the vine and the pumpkin) with a sharp knife. Pull a long strip of absorbent cloth (a wick) through the slit. Put the other end in a glass of water and keep the glass full. The extra water is drawn through the wick into the pumpkin and increases its growth.

SMALL BOYS' HALLOWE'EN PARTY

Boys are restless at parties. They like action and noise and lots of food. These Hallowe'en party suggestions are for boys aged about 5 to 10. The games are active, the food is simple.

GAMES
List the games the children are to play on a big cardboard scoreboard with names across the top. Score 10 points for each winner. Arrange for each child to get a small prize.
- *Peanut hunt:* This ice breaker is so popular that you should hide twice as many peanuts as seems adequate.
- *Obstacle race:* The object is to make the best possible time over a course of obstacles—sawhorses to climb over and under, big cartons to jump through, a balance board. The resources of your garage or playroom determine the extent of this game.
- *Nailing contest:* Supply two teams with hammers, a can of nails, and a big stump from your fireplace supply. The idea is to see which team can pound the most nails *straight* into the stump. Each boy hammers one nail, then lets next team member have a chance. This game needs an adult referee to enforce rules and to be sure all the onlookers stay out of hammer range.
- *Shopping bag race:* The boys stand side by side, each with a heavy shopping bag with string handles. At the signal, they spring into their bags and hop toward the goal. The sacks don't last long, but the noise is highly satisfactory.
- *Three-legged race:* This game slows the boys down a little and gets them in the mood for lunch. Use old sheet strips to tie the boys' "inside" legs together.

LUNCH
While you are preparing lunch—familiar favorites of hamburgers or hot dogs, plenty of milk, potato chips, small bowls of relishes, mustard, catsup, and cupcakes or ice cream in paper cups to be eaten outside—allow the boys to make placemats in pumpkin shapes from orange construction paper. Or, free-for-all crayon decorating of a plain white paper tablecloth is interesting to even the most unartistic.

"TRICK-OR-TREAT"

Since the traditional "trick-or-treat" is today's most popular Hallowe'en activity, it is shrewd to prepare in advance for the invasion of neighborhood children. Present Hallowe'en fun is probably a relic of peasant festivals when nightlong merrymakers fortified themselves with harvest fruit.

As this holiday is principally a children's day, the youngsters usually enjoy helping prepare the treats. Perhaps their role can be as simple as wrapping popcorn balls in bright cellophane. Or placing candy, fruit, or nuts in waxed sandwich bags. Or decorating tiny white bags purchased at a bakery with jack-o'-lanterns and black cats.

Older children can assist in baking these simple cookies for trick-or-treat callers.

Cake Mix Cookies
½ cup (1 cube) butter or margarine
1 egg yolk
1 package yellow cake mix

Cream butter until soft. Add yolk and blend well. Sprinkle in cake mix and beat with mixer turned to medium for 5 minutes, or until crumbly. Turn out on floured board and knead 10 seconds. Roll out to ¼-inch thickness and cut into shapes. Place on ungreased cooky sheet, bake in moderate oven (375°) for 15 minutes. Makes 3½ dozen.

Or, roll dough into balls before baking. Then brush baked cookies with orange icing, adding a citron snip for pumpkin stem.

If you have older children who no longer care to join the yearly raid for treats, have them set up a refreshment stand on the porch. Each caller gets a small paper cup of cider and instructions to place the cup in a nearby wastebasket.

Paper pulp over molded cardboard builds up brow, nose, mouth. Mask can also be used as a wall decoration.

HOW TO MAKE A PAPIER-MÂCHÉ MASK

A startling party mask is easy to make from papier mâché. Slash edges of an oval-shaped piece of corrugated cardboard. For a face shape, dampen it and mold it over a bowl.

Paper pulp is made by combining torn bits of newspaper and a cup of flour paste. (Add two parts hot water to one part flour and cook for a few minutes. Make paste fairly runny.) Papier mâché should be thick enough to handle easily. Build up features with cardboard and cover with a layer of pulp. Smooth edges and cut eye and nose openings. Use poster paint to get strong colors and decorate with a bold beard of raffia or yarn.

Bold design, jutting features, and strong poster paint help to make mask easy to see in Hallowe'en darkness.

WARDROBE IDEAS FOR YOUNG GOBLINS

Young children love to make their own costumes from old clothing, scraps of material, or worn sheets. You can supply the finishing touches after the celebrants have decked themselves out in these easily made costumes.

• *Dress up:* This is for the pre-school or kindergarten child. Let the children select what they wish to wear from a collection of old clothing. Plenty of safety pins will help hike up trailing skirts or big-waisted pants. A touch of poster paint make-up is harmless. Or use breakfast cocoa if the child wants to smudge his face, "hobo" fashion.

• *Pirate:* Fringe the edge of blue jeans cut off just below the knee. A striped T-shirt, bright head scarf, and black eye patch complete the outfit along with a hoop earring and a cardboard cutlass.

• *Gypsy:* Girls can decorate their skirts with glued-on sequins or crepe paper flowers attached with tape.

• *Ghost or skeleton:* Dye an old pair of pajamas black. Mark on ribs with chalk or white poster paint. For an

especially ghastly ghost, stick colored fluorescent tape to an old sheet to make the ribs—they'll glow in the dark!

• *Indian:* Cut armholes in a huge brown paper bag or make a bag from wide wrapping paper. Slit top opening so it is large enough to fit over child's head. Fringe the bottom of the bag and decorate the dress with "Indian" designs. Use chalk, crayon, or poster paint. For a headband, staple cardboard feathers to a cloth strip. Paint a cylindrical oatmeal box for a drum.

• *Robot man:* Cut holes, large enough to fit child's arms and legs, in sides and bottoms of cardboard box. Cut hole in top to fit head. So that the child will be able to get into the suit, slash open one side of the box. Cut eye, mouth, and nose openings in a smaller box which fits over the

head. To make antennas, curl two pieces of wire into a spiral and staple them to top of box. Spray the costume with silver paint.

• *Masks:* Brown paper bags make simple, effective, comfortable masks. Even small children can decorate their own with poster paint and cut out holes for eyes.

Northwest totems — cardboard cartons "with legs" — include a Southwest Indian kachina (second from the left).

TWO-LEGGED TOTEM POLES

Materials: Carton, poster paint, 1-inch brushes, stapler, chalk, tape, cutting tool, book on Indian designs.

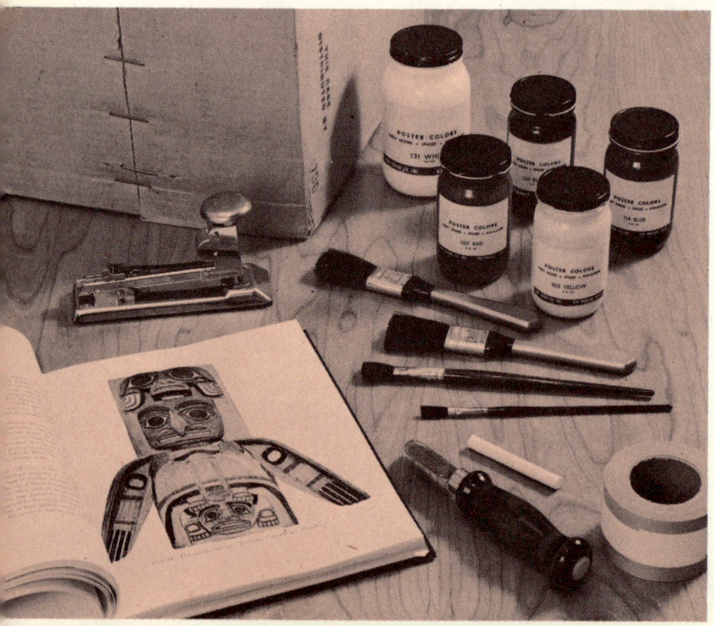

Mother can chalk in the design on the carton; children can help paint and later attach beaks and wings.

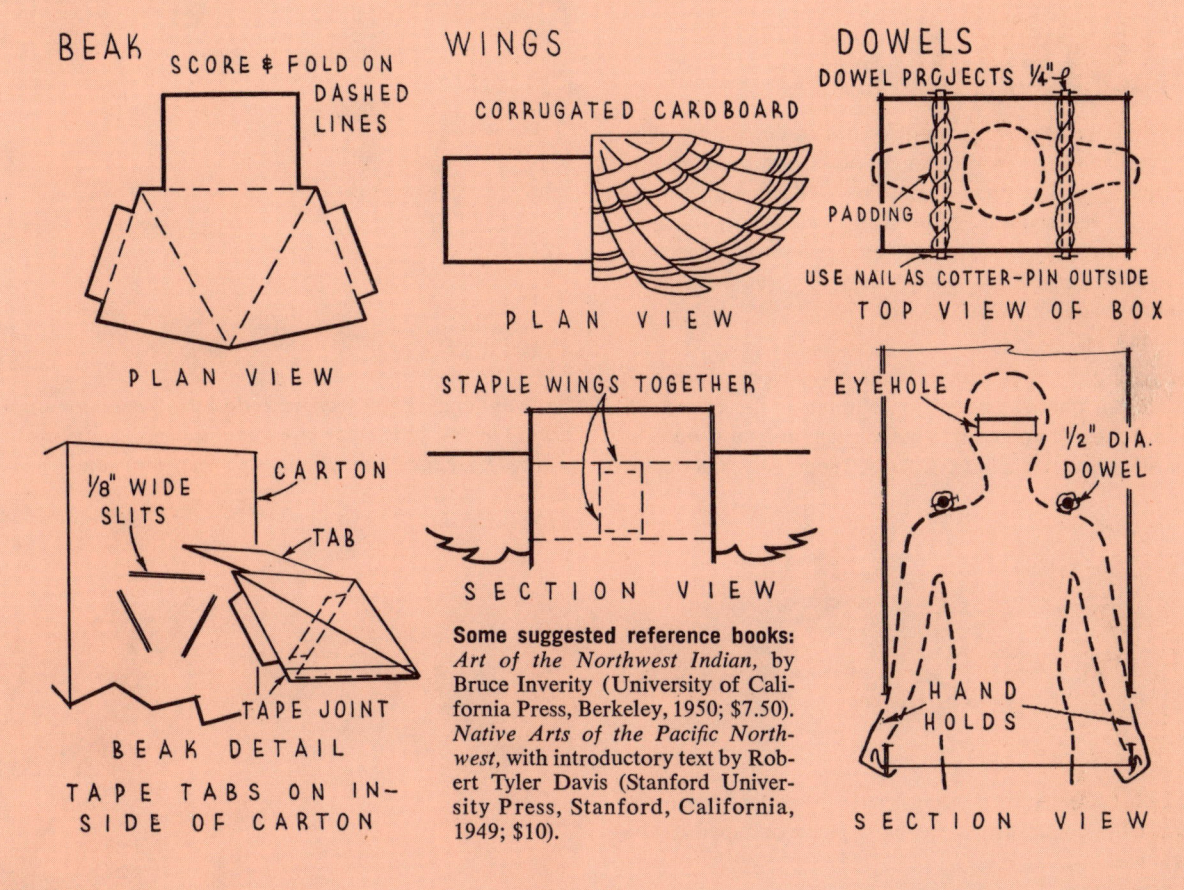

Wouldn't it be fun to see a whole forest of totem poles swaying up the sidewalk on Hallowe'en? Camouflaged with authentic Indian designs, these "animated totems" are tall cartons which completely disguise the neighborhood children.

Large cartons are usually available at grocery or hardware stores. The commercial printing on the box would probably show through your painted designs, so dismantle the carton, lay it flat, and sketch in the designs on the blank side. If you paint the box with the panels flat, reassemble with gummed tape before adding beaks and wings. These features are made from large pieces of cardboard inserted through slits in the boxes and fastened on the inside with staples and tape.

Hand holds are cut about 2 inches up from the bottom of each side. Next, sheet-padded dowels are fastened inside the boxes at shoulder height. These supports make the boxes manageable even in a high wind.

Library books on Northwest Indian art will suggest many colorful patterns.

Hand holds, eyehole are cut with razor. Dowels are padded, inserted at shoulder height for good control.

EASTER IDEAS

Children are creative when it comes to decorating eggs. Just provide them with enough interesting material and dye the eggs. Let them create fancy effects with sewing box supplies—sequins, glitter, fringe, rick-rack, feathers. Apply with rubber cement. Colored legal seals, hole reinforcers, and picture labels are easy to apply because of gummed backing.

CUT-OUTS

Decorating the eggs with cut-outs made from paper (see the bottom photo) and ribbon eliminates the chance of spilling dyes. If you wish to use the eggs as a table decoration, stick them on a base. Cut out 2-inch circles of paper.

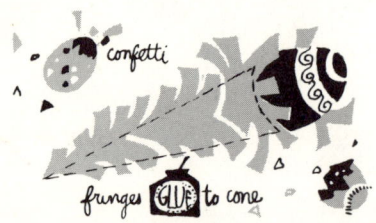

Make a collar from a ⅜-inch strip of paper. Place the egg on the collar which has been glued or taped to the circle base.

CASCARON

A Mexican *cascaron* (shell) favor is fun for both children and adults. According to tradition, at the height of a Mexican festival, those who have *cascarones* break them over the head of a friend, showering him with colored confetti.

To prepare a *cascaron*, blow the egg out of the shell. (Pierce both ends of egg with darning needle, making bottom hole larger than top. Blow egg through opening.) Fill egg loosely with confetti through larger hole; tape over hole. Form a stiff paper cone 7 inches long with a mouth big enough to hold a third of the egg. Tape egg in place. Decorate cone with bows, fringe, or loops made from tissue paper. Paint designs on top of the egg with water colors.

Blow out eggs. Paint free-hand designs (using fine-tipped brush) over a base color of enamel which has dried overnight. Dry eggs on meat sticks pushed into sand.

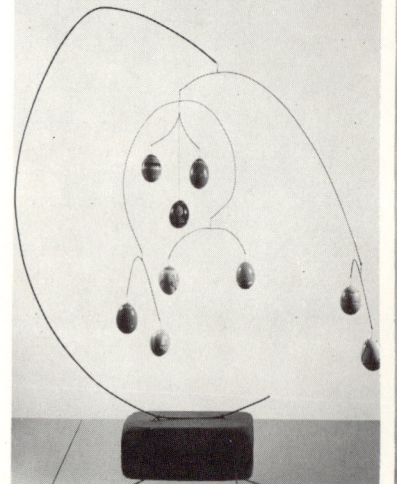 

Left: Whimsical mobile made from blown-out eggs suspended by thread from slender wires that are fastened to heavier "base" wire. Right: Poster paint sepals and pipe cleaner stems make egg flowers for "potted plant."

Bottle cap taped to cardboard brim is man's hat; ruffled crepe paper forms lady's headpiece; bunny's whiskers are made of paper and attached with a straight pin.

THE HUNT

Dramatize the hunt as much as possible. Plan the event on unfamiliar territory—a park or a friend's ranch. Before hiding the eggs, tape on pennies or nickels. For toddling first-timers, tape eggs at various intervals along the ribbon. The long ribbon is then wound along a maze-like course, disappearing into a flower pot or plant each time an egg is hidden. To avoid too many after-Easter eggs, wrap small gifts (pencils, comb, toothbrush) and hide them. Peanuts in the shell make another good substitute.

Salt carton bunny is covered with white paper. Draw features with crayon. Pink paper ears fit in slits in box top. Add black tie, ruffled crepe paper collar.

FOOD SUGGESTIONS

- *Peanut-butter chick-wiches:* From peanut butter sandwiches cut circles with biscuit cutter. Thin carrot strips are legs, a small circle of cheese is the head. Chick has raisin beak, and 3 raisins are skewered on a toothpick for a jaunty tail.
- *Bunny burger:* On the cooked meat patty make dill pickle ears, carrot stick whiskers, olive ring eyes, and catsup mouth.
- *Egg nest salad:* Arrange nest of shredded salad greens on plates. Fill each nest with thawed frozen yellow cantaloup balls, pale honeydew balls, peach balls, pink-tinted pear balls.

THIS RABBIT COMES ON EASTER MORNING

This little girl found Mr. Easter Bunny himself on her treasure hunt. Rabbit's head is full of surprises.

Collect tiny gifts. Wrap one in a strip of crepe paper; keep adding presents and paper until ball is head size.

Tape on cardboard ears; add several layers of white crepe paper and paint the face. For whiskers, twist five pipe cleaners together at one end; poke them into the rabbit's cheeks. Stand the head in a cardboard ring.

Thanksgiving table for children is harvest-bright with a turkey place card and a nut-and-candy dish at each place.

Center of the table is decorated with paper pumpkins and a cornucopia filled with fruit and nuts.

PAPER SCULPTURES... FOR A CHILDREN'S THANKSGIVING

If you seat the children at a separate table at Thanksgiving, make it a special table — gay with harvest colors, turkey place-cards, paper pumpkins, and a cornucopia spilling over with fruit and nuts.

All favors are made of a good grade of construction paper in autumn colors. Staple, glue, or tape the pieces together.

Here are some working tips: It is easier to fold or roll paper parallel to the grain. Determine the grain by folding a piece of paper. If folded against the grain, it will crack; along the grain, it will fold into a sharp crease.

• *Curling:* Curl a cylinder by pulling paper lightly down over a table edge with grain parallel to the edge.

• *Scoring:* Thin paper can be folded by hand, parallel to the grain. Score heavier papers. Scoring cuts the fibers so

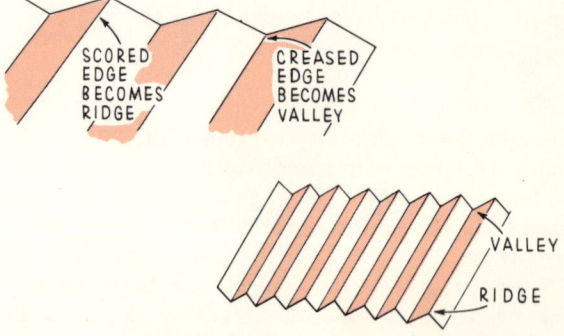

paper can be folded in any direction. Use pen knife or single-edged razor blade, and a metal ruler as guide. To accordion-pleat, fold one pleat and use it as a guide for the rest.

PUMPKIN

(1) Cut a 3 by 7-inch piece of paper. (2) Pencil in overlap line. (3) Roll and fasten cylinder. (4) Cut a 6 by 7-inch piece. Score vertical lines 1 inch in from each 6-inch edge. (5) With ruler, mark slots in paper every ½ inch parallel to 7-inch side. Stop at vertical lines. (6) Fold paper on scored lines. (7) Insert tabs in cylinder and tape. *Top:* Cut 3-inch square of paper; score as indicated: (8) diagonal lines on face side, (9) dotted lines on the reverse side. (10) Reverse back to face side and push down center. Attach to pumpkin with glue.

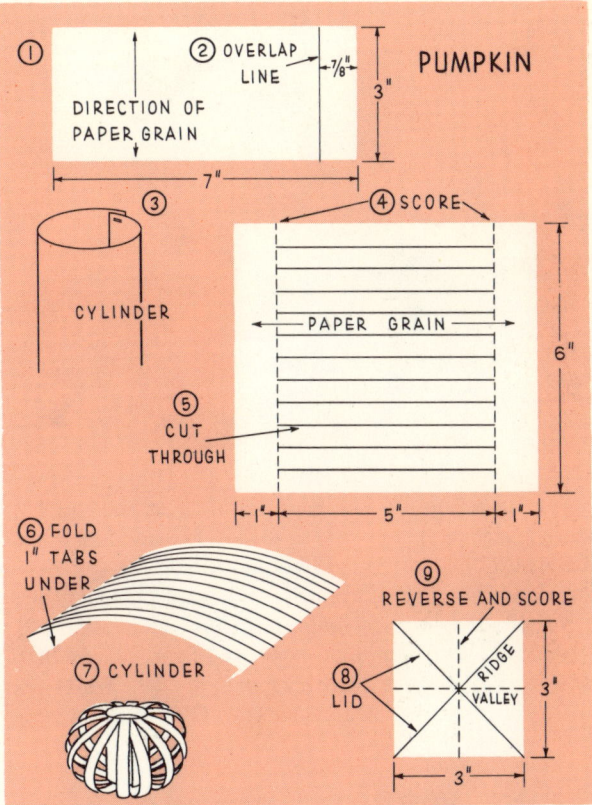

TURKEY PLACE CARD

Tail: (1) Accordion-pleat two 5½ by 4-inch papers. Fold parallel to 4-inch side every ⅜ inch. (2) Crease, spread fanwise. (3-4-5) Fasten as indicated. *Body:* (6) Score, fold a 4-inch square diagonally. (7) Reverse, score line indicated. (8) Cut diagonal to score line. (9) Bend triangles out for tail. (10) Cut out triangle on fold for neck. (11) Fold down corner for head. (12) Attach tail. *Stand:* (13) Score and fold lengthwise a 4 by 8-inch paper. (14) Cut slots indicated. (15) Stick turkey legs in slots.

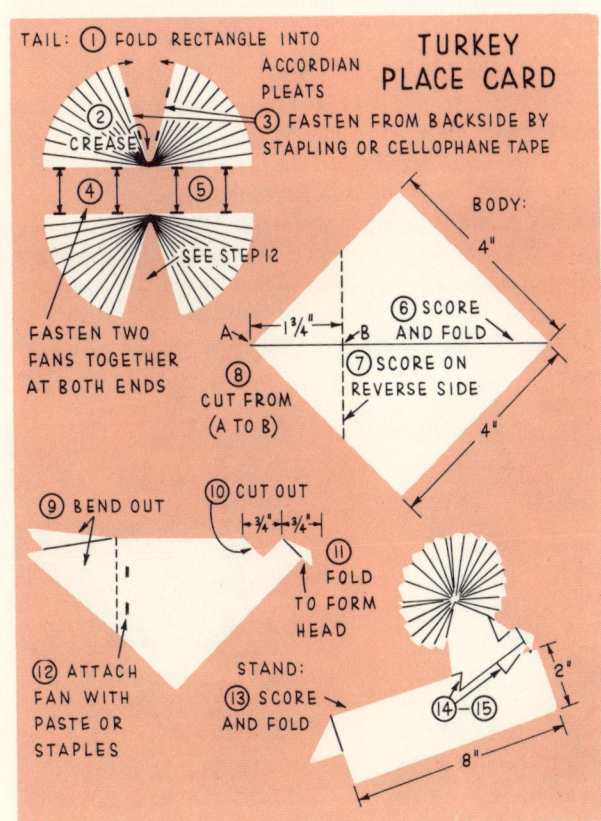

13

NUT-AND-CANDY DISH

Base: Cut a 2 by 12-inch paper; starting at one end (1) score a vertical line every 2½ inches, leaving 2-inch tab. Reverse; (2) score dotted lines indicated. (3) Cut from top down to apex of triangle. (4) Bend "collars" out. (5) Fold along vertical lines, form box, and fasten tab. *Dish:* Use 5-inch square of paper. (6) Score perpendicular lines. (7) Reverse, score diagonal lines. (8) Turn back to face side, push down center. (9) Glue dish on base as shown.

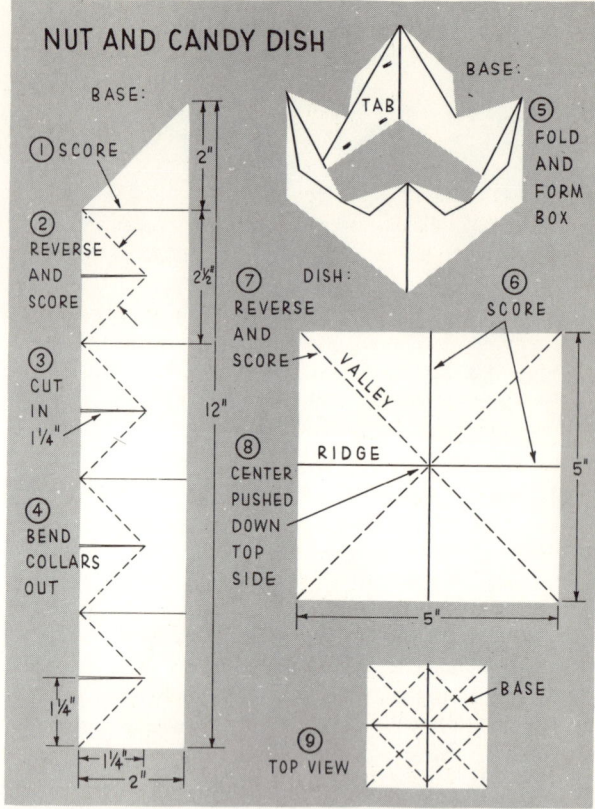

CORNUCOPIA AND PEDESTAL

Cornucopia: Use 12-inch square of heavy construction paper. (1) Rule vertical lines 1 inch in from each edge. (2) With metal-edged ruler, slit paper horizontally (with grain) every ½ inch; stop at vertical lines. (3) Bring corners A and B together and staple. *Pedestal:* For base, use 4 by 18-inch strip of paper. (4) Score vertically every 4 inches along 18-inch side, leaving 2-inch tab; fold and fasten. Make the top (5), (6), same as candy dish top. (7) Place on top of base.

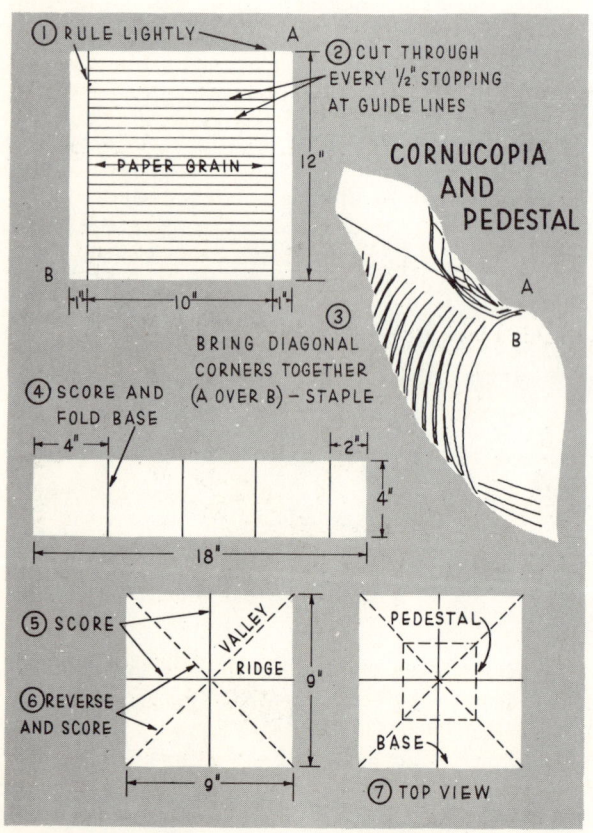

NEW YEAR'S EVE PARTY FUN

There is a special trick in holding a New Year's Eve party for children. Keep the affair and preparations really simple so that you won't be too tired for the adult activity later.

Most younger children will accept the idea of celebrating early. Noisemakers, streamers, and horns will signal the time for the end of the party—long before midnight! These suggestions are for children 10 to 12.

UNTRIMMING PARTY
Have a fire brightly crackling in your fireplace when the guests arrive. You will use the coals later for roasting apples. Serve a very lazy supper—fruit juice and crackers,

soup and sandwiches. Then invite the guests to help untrim the Christmas tree. Be sure that you have removed your favorite fragile ornaments ahead of time. Have plenty of boxes and a supply of tissue for wrapping.

If you wish, arrange that each child take home an ornament for his own family tree next year. Or hang wrapped favors labeled with each guest's name on the tree.

When the tree is bare, ask an adult to carry it outside and cut off the top 2 or 3 feet. While the tree is being cut, let each child wrap a cored apple, raisin-filled, in aluminum foil. Place apples in the fireplace in the low-burning coals. Turn several times during the 35-minute baking time.

Meanwhile, bring in the tree top and hang it upside-down in a doorway. Let the children attach food to the tree so it can be a New Year's bird feeder. Apple cores and scraps of suet, tied in small mesh bags or pushed into tiny pine cones, are good choices for the birds. (You may bring the tree outside at once or leave it in the house until the next day.) Now serve the still-firm warm apples on plates; pass a large shaker with cinnamon-sugar.

PAPER BAG SKITS
Give each team—three guests to a team—a paper bag containing three objects to be used in a short skit. You might give one team a roller skate, a ribbon, a tennis ball;

to another, a cup, an umbrella, a scarf. Give each team about five minutes to plan its skit. Older children especially enjoy these paper bag dramatics.

FORTUNES
Fortune telling is traditional on New Year's Eve. Older children will probably enjoy this game. Pass out sheets of white paper folded lengthwise. On the opened sheets place a blob of poster paint on the crease. Use a different color for each person, if possible. Have each person refold his paper and gently press the halves together so that the paint spreads out freely inside. Carefully open papers.

While the paint dries, clip each child's name to his paper square. Pass the papers around the group one at a time, first removing the name slip. Ask each child to tell what he sees in the painted shape. After the paper has been all the way around, tell whose paper it is. The things that have been "seen" indicate that child's fortune.

ST. PATRICK'S DAY BIRTHDAY PARTY

If there is a birthday to celebrate or if you just feel that children *need* a mid-March party, St. Patrick's Day provides a theme or good excuse for festivity. Here is a luncheon lineup that befits the occasion.

•

MENU
Fresh Fruits on Sticks
Shamrock Tuna in Patty Shells
Carrot Sticks   Potato Chips   Ripe Olives
Individual Birthday Cakes
Ice Cream "Cake" with Candles
Limeade

•

• *Fresh Fruits on Sticks.* At each place put a large raw *Irish* potato, bristling with orange sections, cubes of apple, pear, and pineapple. Impale a maraschino cherry, too.

•

• *Shamrock Tuna in Patty Shells.* Simple creamed tuna in bakery or homemade patty shells. Adorn tops with shamrocks cut from green peppers. Make a paper shamrock as a cutting guide.

•

• *Individual Birthday Cakes.* Young children like this idea, for each gets a cake with his own name on it and a candle to blow out when the host blows out those on the big ice cream cake. Use your favorite mix; bake in cupcake pans lined with fluted green papers. Frost with green icing. Use commercial plastic-tube white icing to write the names.

•

• *Ice Cream "Cake."* Pack vanilla ice cream into a deep cake pan or spring form. Place in freezer for a few hours. Unmold on cake plate and decorate with swirls of green-tinted whipped cream. Stick in candles. Also write "Happy Birthday to - - - - -" on the ice cream. Return to freezer before serving.

Two young swashbucklers read the charred invitation that brought them to the party.

Outdoor lunch is served to hungry pirates. "Treasure chest" is sheet cake on box (you could also stack several layers of cake).

A PARTY FOR SWASHBUCKLING PIRATES

Chances are that any 7 to 10-year-old boys at your house would be good candidates for a pirate party. The plans are simple enough—just some easy costumes, a treasure hunt, and a hearty lunch for Captain Kidd and crew.

The host will enjoy helping make invitations. Char edges of brown paper. Crudely print the place, date, time, and order to wear blue jeans.

When the guests arrive, outfit them with pirate gear—colored bandannas, eye patches of black paper and twill tape, large rings of cardboard to hang over ears for earrings. Mark on mustaches and whiskers with eyebrow pencil. Gird the boys with bright sashes.

Organize the treasure hunt before lunch. Give each boy clues written on scraps of paper resembling an ancient map. Make the clues progressive—"under a tree, 10 paces north, turn right," and so forth. The treasure—mesh bags filled with gold foil-wrapped chocolate coins—might be buried in a tin can beneath a tree.

After the hunt, serve lunch, colorful with "pirate food" such as this:

Ship's Biscuits: Cornbread squares filled with ham and cheese. *Pirate Gold Salad:* Raisin and carrot salad mixed with mayonnaise and peanut butter. *Pirate Jewels:* Pickles, olives and radishes. *Cannon Balls:* Small scoops of vanilla and chocolate ice cream. *Treasure Chest Cake:* Chocolate frosted cake with yellow-icing hinges, bindings, and lock. Mount sheet cake on brown painted box (same size as cake).

After lunch the pirates may wish to sail off in ships made of large cardboard cartons or packing cases with good sized cut-out port holes. Swords can be cut from cardboard or other safe material.

Buy or borrow an old-fashioned crank freezer and treat your children to one of the joys of your own childhood.

These youngsters — each having helped with the cranking — take special delight in licking fresh peach cones.

ICE CREAM... FROM A CRANK FREEZER

It's not just nostalgia for the "good old days" that makes crank-freezer ice cream so wonderful. Freezer ice cream still *is* wonderful! Fresh fruits, cream, eggs, and hard work are the magic ingredients.

Children of all ages will delight in helping you make it, and will compete for the right to lick the dasher. Try to give each child a job — preparing fruit, crushing ice, or cranking the freezer.

Here's the procedure:

1. Pour ice cream mixture into freezer can, about two-thirds full, and chill thoroughly.
2. Crush ice as fine as possible.
3. Adjust dasher in can. Cover can with wax paper and put on the freezer can cover securely.
4. Fit can into freezer, adjust frame and crank, and tighten screws.
5. Measure ice and salt. Use 1 part rock salt to 8 parts ice; or, ½ cup salt for each quart of ice. Tamp down first quart of ice evenly in freezer. Then alternate salt and ice until full. A 2-quart freezer will take 4 quarts of crushed ice and 2 cups (1 pound) of ice cream salt.
6. Start cranking and continue until the dasher is very hard to turn. About 15 minutes is average.
7. Drain off surplus water. Unfasten the screws and remove crank and frame. Remove top layers of ice. Carefully wipe top and sides so that no salt will get into the ice cream. Remove top and slowly lift dasher.
8. The children probably will want the ice cream served immediately. Or "mellow" it for an hour or two the old-fashioned way.

Cover the can with a piece of wax paper, replace top, and plug dasher hole with a cork. Add ice and double proportion of salt to freezer until can is covered. Blanket it with newspapers or burlap and let it sit.

This is the basic recipe for various flavored ice creams.

VANILLA ICE CREAM
3-inch piece of vanilla bean pod **or**
1½ teaspoons vanilla
1½ cups milk
1 tablespoon cornstarch
¼ teaspoon salt
¾ cup sugar
4 egg yolks
1½ cups whipping cream

Split vanilla pod and scrape seed into milk; drop in the pod. (Or add vanilla to milk.) Scald. Combine cornstarch, salt, sugar, and slightly beaten egg yolks; mix well. Beat in a little of the scalded milk, then combine the two mixtures and cook over a low heat, stirring constantly, until thick and smooth. Chill, then stir in cream and pour into freezer can. Makes a generous quart.

•

PEACH ICE CREAM
Follow the Vanilla Ice Cream recipe, but substitute ¾ teaspoon almond extract for the vanilla. Add 1½ cups fresh ripe peeled peaches, mashed through a strainer. The yield is 1½ quarts.

•

Crushed peppermint sticks make this a pretty pink ice cream.

PEPPERMINT STICK ICE CREAM
Follow recipe for Vanilla Ice Cream, with these changes: Reduce sugar to ¼ cup and add 1 cup coarsely crushed peppermint sticks. Makes 1¼ quarts.

•

Shavings of chocolate—the favorite of most children—fleck this light flavored ice cream.

CHOCOLATE FLAKE ICE CREAM
In basic Vanilla Ice Cream recipe make these changes: Reduce sugar to ½ cup. Add 1 cup of shaved sweet or semi-sweet chocolate. Makes 1¼ quarts.

As party starts, all the guests get very busy putting decorations on paper bags, using crayons provided as favors. When everyone has finished, awards are made for fanciest, funniest, most original.

TO GET A PARTY ROLLING...

Bags and crayons ready for guests. Bias tape handles are fastened with transparent tape, stapled to bag. Prizes and favors go into bags as the party progresses. Each guest takes loot bag home.

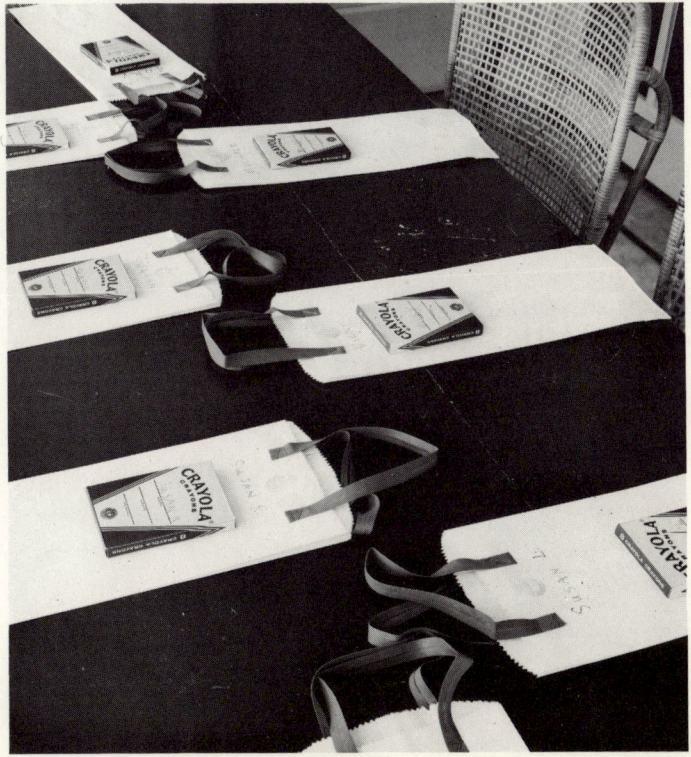

"Help yourself" can be the rule even for three-year-olds at an outdoor party. Jug is set within easy reach.

Children like the freedom of an outdoor party. Wide open spaces allow great variety of games and free play.

Sandwich lunch is packed in name-labeled bags for easy serving. Favors may also be included in the sacks.

Four containers—picnic hamper, ice cream carton, vacuum jug, wire laundry basket—hold everything for party.

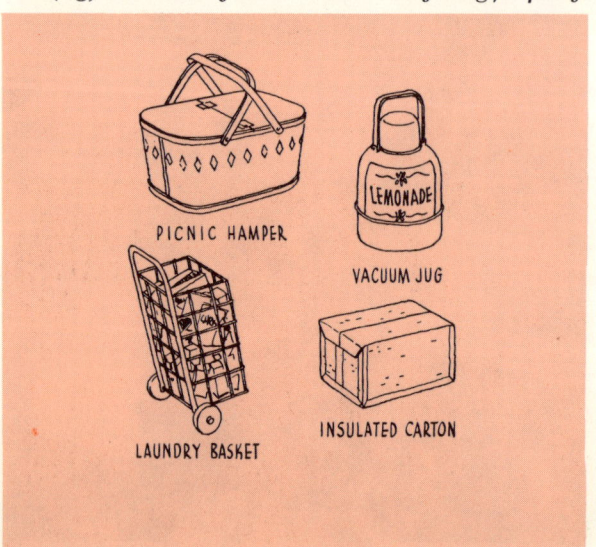

CHILDREN LOVE A BIRTHDAY PICNIC

The birthday picnic for children — especially pre-schoolers — has many advantages over the birthday party at home. Adults do have to supervise, of course, but not so much as with the same number of children at home. As nearly everything used is disposable, there is little worry about breakage and cleaning up after the party ends.

A birthday in the park can have as much "party" atmosphere as you wish. A wire laundry basket on wheels holds favors, prizes, table decorations, and presents the guests have brought. The all-important item — the ice cream — is packed in a carton of dry ice.

Pack individual lunches: half a peanut butter sandwich and half a chopped egg sandwich, carrot sticks, a napkin or paper bib. These go into a picnic hamper along with a small cake (to serve the mothers who also come), a cupcake and 3-inch candle for each child, flat-bottomed ice cream cones, and animal crackers to push into the ice cream.

Also into the hamper go the essential miscellaneous items — large checked tablecloth (the breeze may disturb the traditional paper one and cause too much hilarity), knife for cutting cake, ice cream scoop, and damp washcloths in a plastic bag.

A large vacuum jug with a spigot holds a gallon of lemonade, made from four cans of frozen lemonade concentrate. Even very young children can help themselves if this container is placed in a low spot.

After the gifts are opened, round up the little guests and get them home in time for naps.

EACH GIRL BRINGS HER FAVORITE DOLL

A "party within a party" is often a successful formula for 7-year-old girls because it gives a good reason to bring their dolls along, too. Have the invitations read: "Come to a birthday luncheon and bring your favorite small doll." Later, in newly acquired finery made by the girls during the afternoon, the dolls have their own party and little cakes.

After gifts are opened, lunch is served: soup and sandwiches, vegetable sticks and cottage cheese, milk, birthday cake, and ice cream.

Next, the girls fashion costumes for their dolls from several colors of crepe paper. Each package is cut crosswise into thirds before the party. The trimmings you provide are most important as they add elegance to the dresses: sequins, rick-rack, gold braid, fringe, artificial flowers, feathers. Hold them in place with glue and thread.

Dressed-up dolls have their own party. Bake miniature cakes in tiny fluted cups from a candy shop. Fit 2 cups together for each cake, place on baking sheet, and spoon 1 teaspoon cake batter in each; bake 15 minutes at 375°.

After lunch, girls dress their favorite dolls in crepe paper costumes for "dolls' party" which will climax the birthday event.

Seven-year-olds find crepe paper easy to sew and to decorate with glued-on lace, ribbons.

Several mothers are needed to put finishing touches on costumes and to thread needles.

Fishing party: Ribbon guides child from place setting to gift tucked between cake layers. Fish kites hint of game to follow. Molded fruit ring, cottage cheese, carrot curls, sandwiches, and ginger ale complete the meal.

PLAN THE PARTY AROUND A THEME

Most parents don't need to be reminded that there is no standard kind of successful birthday party. A child is partial to a different type of celebration at various stages in his development. Generally, however, children do prefer that the party be planned around a meal. Here are a few suggestions — to serve only as guideposts — for handling birthday parties, with special emphasis on coordinating the food with the party theme and activities.

FISHING PARTY

With children from 3 to 5, you must carefully plan and organize *all* activities. The very young like food of the type they get at home, served at the usual times. Social events need not last long as naps are still important to some and excitement runs rather high.

This is an age when children often judge the success of a party by the number of things they may take home. Provide them with paper sacks for extra pieces of cake and for favors.

Always good for pre-schoolers is a game of fish after lunch. As part of the table decorations, use two Japanese paper fish kites (available in many variety and dime stores) puffed out with tissue paper, to give a clue to the game which will follow.

Fasten a sheet at adult head height across the doorway to a small room. Children take turns fishing over the sheet with a bamboo rod or a broom handle to which a long piece of string is tied. When they drop the line behind the sheet, tie on a gaily wrapped gift — pencil, notebook, balloon — and give the line a jerk. Allow each little guest a chance to fish two or three times. See that the children leave while they are still excited about their catch.

DECORATING PARTY

This small party, planned for six girls, satisfies their urge to make things and use utensils. Bake a large cake to serve with lunch, consisting of fruit salad, creamed chicken, popovers, and milk. Also make a small loaf cake for each girl. On a large table arrange cakes, decorating tubes, colored frosting, and ornamental candy. Let each girl decorate her own cake to take home in a bakery box. Large round cookies provide a chance to practice.

OUTDOOR PARTY

Weather permitting, a back yard, beach, or public park is an ideal locale for the activities of the 8 to 10-year-olds. Pack each dinner in a paper paint bucket, available from most paint stores. The menu could include fried chicken, potato salad, relishes, and fruit. Or the children may wish to cook hot dogs on a stick over a barbecue. Add gay red and white checked napkins. For a dramatic, wind-resistant blaze on the cake, try sparklers.

EXPLORATION PARTY

Children from 4 to 10 like sightseeing trips — to a nearby ranch, airport, or fire station. (Be sure to ask permission ahead of time.) This type of party is easiest to handle when there are only four or five guests. Serve a familiar lunch of meat loaf, green beans, and scalloped potatoes before you go exploring. Cake and favors in the photo offer a clue to the surprise — a visit to a farm. Paper plates and paper cloth can be discarded when festivities have ended.

CHUCKWAGON PARTY

For a mixed group of teen-agers, the informality of a chuckwagon buffet "breaks the ice." Here again the hamburger and hot dog, with all their trimmings, reign. Tamale pie, baked beans, or spaghetti will help take care of the enormous appetite of this age group. Keep ice cream firm in a pan of cracked ice and salt. Provide nuts, cherries, coconut, and sauces (here a Lazy-Susan can come in handy). Make an oversized table of planks set across wooden sawhorses.

BIRTHDAY TABLECLOTH

A birthday history tablecloth could be the entertainment highlight of a little girl's birthday party each year. Before the child's first party, select an inexpensive white cloth or even a sheet. All guests (or parents) are asked to sign or draw on the cloth. Before laundering, all markings are embroidered over with colored floss. This is done each year. (Embroidering will not be necessary if you let the children write with crayons, then iron the cloth with a hot iron *before* you wash it so the crayon "sets.")

The children have great fun finding their previous marks — and seeing gradual changes in their writing. As soon as the party dishes are cleared away, a new area to be written on is blocked off and the girls go to work.

Especially in the 7 to 9-year bracket, youngsters show a lively spirit of competition, each trying to make the best drawing or write the most amusing greeting.

Birthday guest carefully signs her name on tablecloth while other girls attentively wait their turn to write.

Signatures and drawings on cloth are embroidered over in colored floss before laundering, to save through years.

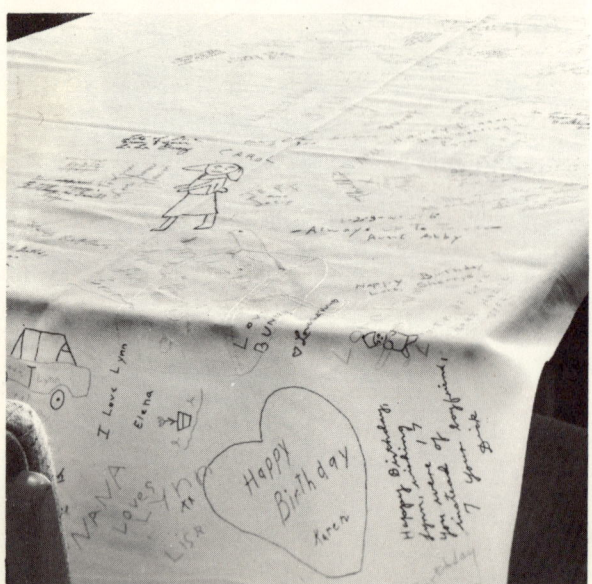

GIANT SNOW CAKE

A giant snow cake is a novel way to celebrate a child's winter birthday if you live in snowy country. Or plan it as a climax of a weekend trip to the mountains.

Here are suggestions for building the snow cake: Beforehand, waterproof gift packages by wrapping them in plastic. While the birthday child is occupied elsewhere, gather the group at a chosen spot to build the jumbo "cake." Pile the wrapped packages into a mound and pack loose snow around them to shape the cake. When it is about 3 feet high, sculpture scalloped "icing" with mittened hands. Top with icicles and large candles. At dusk, light candles and surprise the birthday child. Suggest that he slice his cake with a shovel to discover his gifts. When they are found, move indoors for supper and opening of gifts by the fireplace.

FREEZER FARE

Once in a while, impromptu parties are the most fun of all. Keep your freezer stocked with simple fixings and you will be all set for guests in lots of one or a dozen.

Make up everything ahead on a day when you have extra time. Freeze it and reheat when needed. Hot dogs, still frozen, will go right into a big kettle to heat. The buns come out of the freezer a half hour before serving to thaw in their wrappings. Fruit juice or punch concentrate is mixed in minutes.

To make an ice cream cake, put ice cream between two layers of cake and freeze on a cooky sheet. When frozen solid, decorate with frosting, perhaps colored whipped cream. Add a "Happy Birthday" message, if you wish. Replace cake in freezer to harden frosting. Store until 5 or 10 minutes before serving.

Young cowboys arriving for party are given a string of event tickets in exchange for the admission ticket which was also the invitation.

WESTERN RODEO PARTY

If your son is between 7 and 10 years of age, he undoubtedly would enjoy a Western rodeo birthday party. Boys especially, and some girls, enjoy this type of event.

INVITATIONS
Cut invitations from construction paper to look like admission tickets. Type in the name and place of Robert's or Jimmy's Rodeo. The ticket stubs can be used for a draw prize awarded at the party's climax. Be sure that each ticket is a different color.

TICKET AND SOUVENIR BOOTHS
Set up two orange crate booths labeled TICKETS and SOUVENIRS. In return for his admission ticket each guest gets a string of event tickets to be used at the games and chuck wagon meal to follow. Print these on construction paper and use an unthreaded sewing machine to make the tear-off perforations between each of the tickets. Guests then move on to the souvenir stand and receive paper cowboy hats, kerchiefs, or sheriff badges.

RODEO GAMES
Dressed in Western wear, an adult acts as master of ceremonies. He announces when each game is to take place and then directs the event. Start with the most active game first as children usually arrive at a party raring to go.

• *Stage coach race:* Place two chairs 50 to 100 feet from starting point. Guests form two teams, each divided into pairs — horse and driver. At a signal, horse puts a large paper bag over his head and starts toward the chair goal. The driver may steer him by *voice* only — any touching costs driver 2 points. When the pair reaches goal, children switch positions for return trip. First team to get all its members back wins 10 points each.

• *Steer roping:* Place steer head (see below) on the floor and determine a tossing line. Each cowboy has five tries

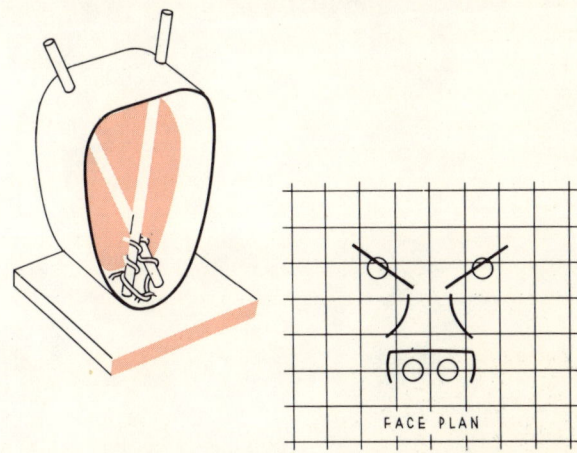

Make steer's head from a large ham can. Poke dowels through top for horns; attach with wire and staples to can bottom and wood stand. Spray-paint; paint on face.

to rope the steer by the horns using deck quoits or other large rings. Allow one point for a ringer.

• *Horse race:* A chair marks the finish line. Boys choose partners — one is the *horse,* the other the *rider.* The rider holds the horse by the ankles and the horse walks on his hands to the finish line. Boys change places and return to the starting line. Winning pair wins 10 points, second wins 9, and so on.

• *Quick draw contest:* Each cowboy uses a gun with rubber tipped dart to shoot at the target. Award 10 points for bull's-eyes, decreasing points for other hits.

For scorekeeping, mark off a large piece of brown paper in sections, with children's names down the side and events across the top. At the end of the party, award grand prize to winner and prizes to all runners-up.

CHOW AT CHUCK WAGON
Guests line up and present their last event ticket for chow at the chuck wagon — a picnic table decorated with paper cloth and napkins with cowboy designs. You could make felt or oilcloth holsters to hold napkins and plastic fork and spoon for each guest. Serve a meal of frankfurters and baked beans, topped off with wagon wheel-decorated birthday cake and cocoa.

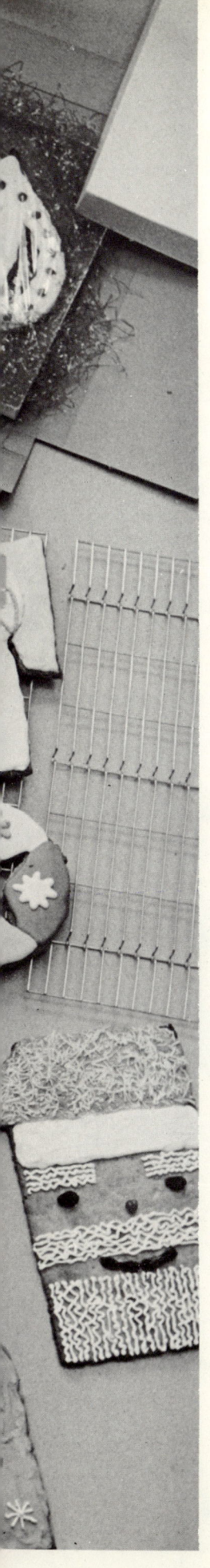

FOR CHRISTMAS... GIANT COOKIES

If a small cooky brings a little pleasure to a child, a big cooky should bring a lot — that's the thought behind these giant Christmas cookies. Some can be "framed" in shallow boxes, "glassed-in" with plastic wrap, and displayed by every child on your list as works of kitchen art before December 25th. And, when they *are* eaten, there is enough cooky in each to supply a whole day of treats for most children!

Two secrets of success in making these sturdy giants lie in choosing designs and recipes that will give you cookies which won't break easily — especially important if any will be mailed. Bulky shapes without protruding parts work best.

The recipe we chose is a chewy fruit and spice combination that improves in flavor as it ages, provided the cookies are properly sealed from the air. They should be kept flat, if possible.

GIANT HONEY SPICE COOKIES
⅔ cup strained honey
1 cup brown sugar, firmly packed
2 eggs
1 teaspoon grated lemon peel
1 tablespoon lemon juice
3 cups flour
½ teaspoon soda
¼ teaspoon salt
½ teaspoon cinnamon
¼ teaspoon **each** ginger and cloves
⅔ cup ground candied orange peel
½ cup ground candied lemon peel
½ cup ground or grated almonds

Bring the honey to a boil in a small saucepan. Remove from heat; add sugar and stir until dissolved. Beat eggs until light and lemon colored; blend in honey and sugar mixture, lemon peel, and lemon juice. Sift and measure flour; sift again with soda, salt, and spices. Add to honey-and-egg mixture along with candied orange peel, lemon peel, and almonds; mix well. Chill at least 4 hours, or overnight.

For each big cooky use about ⅛ of dough. One at a time, roll out a portion of dough ¾ inch thick on a floured board, then place on a well-greased baking sheet (preferably one with only 1 or 2 sides) and continue to roll out until ¼ inch thick. With a small, sharp, floured knife, cut a big cooky, lifting off the edges as you proceed and saving the dough to re-roll.

You can follow a paper pattern that has been dusted with flour, or make your own designs in the dough, or cut big squares or rounds (a coffee can makes an excellent cutter).

Bake in a moderately hot oven (375°) for 12 to 15 minutes or until lightly browned. Slip a spatula under cooky to loosen, let cool a few seconds on baking sheet, then finish cooling on wire racks before decorating. Makes about 8 giant cookies.

ORNAMENTAL FROSTING
3 large egg whites
1 pound (about 4¾ cups) sifted powdered sugar
1 teaspoon vanilla or lemon extract

Whip egg whites until soft peaks form; beat in sugar, add flavoring. Makes about 4 cups white

For giant cookies, cut around paper pattern laid over dough; lift off excess dough as you cut.

frosting. Tint icing with food coloring, adding more sugar or a few drops of water to get the decorating consistency you want. You may find it helpful to trim the cookies assembly-line fashion, using one color frosting at a time. Use either force bag or cake decorators and a knife to apply.

Show off these giants by wrapping individually in shallow boxes, covering the fronts with clear plastic wrap. (Plastic makes a display window and also seals cooky to keep it fresh.) To mail, put lid on box, pack inside mailing box, and cushion well with paper.

WHY NOT MAKE

HISTORY STOCKINGS

To four small boys these stockings aren't just holders for Christmas presents. On each one, there is a symbolic record of that boy's development.

What will be added each year is always a surprise to the children. On Christmas Eve they sit around the fire while the year's highlights are recounted for each child. They all try to guess what has been added to the stocking. Then the stockings are hung to be filled with treasure in the morning.

The stockings are made of red felt about 18 inches long. The cut-outs are felt, sequins, beads, bells. When one side is filled, the "history" is continued on the back.

There is a cut-out of the state where the child was born and a tree for the first Christmas. Such "firsts" as a kite, snowman, turtle, football, a cat, or a train trip are recorded. More recent symbols on the backs of the stockings show a butterfly net, a lawn mower, and a school book.

GREETING CARD RUGS

These "family greeting cards" are inexpensive rugs made or decorated especially for the holiday season. They are put down early in December as the first indication of good times to follow soon.

• *The star rug:* You'll need 1½ yards *each* of gold burlap and white or tan burlap. On paper draw a 4-pointed star 25 inches from tip to tip. Cut out a pair of these and paste one on the other to form an 8-pointed star. Using this pattern, cut 2 gold burlap stars and 2 white or tan ones. Machine-sew the matching pairs together, leaving an opening so you can turn them right side out.

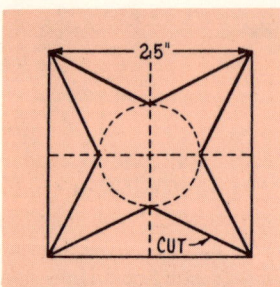

For padding, cut several thicknesses of terry cloth. Stitch together loosely to hold, and slip padding inside white star. Stitch loosely through all thicknesses. Place the white star over the gold so that the combination forms a 16-pointed star. Hand sew at edges to hold. Sew on gold braid in star outline. Attach white chenille balls (cut from ball fringe) to the braid at intervals.

• *The shag rug* (above): Buy a small white cotton throw rug with shallow looping. On the back draw the design, remembering to letter backwards as the design will be reversed on the front of the rug. Use a punch hook, available in needle-work departments, to hook the pattern in bright yarn. Keep the design simple, since you'll have to use more force than usual to punch through the rug's rubberized backing.

A CHRISTMAS TRADITION?

STARCH TREE
Let your children help with this family holiday decoration. You soak yarn in heavy laundry starch to make this lightweight, airy tree. Cover a heavy paper cone with waxed paper and thrust a sewing machine needle through the top. Soak lengths of yarn (twice the height of the cone) in starch. Spiral wet yarn up the cone, first encircling the base five or six times. Then, anchoring yarn firmly to base, lay lengths somewhat diagonally from base to top to base. When absolutely dry, remove tree from form; cut and glue tissue paper "windows" in place from the inside.

TINY PIÑATAS
Fill these little pull-down piñatas with candies or toys for a children's Christmas party. Each piñata is a cup from an egg carton, painted with poster paint in gay Mexican designs. Cut a three-inch fringe of tissue paper and glue it around inside of rim. Tie a knot in the end of a length of yarn and string it through egg cup. Fill cup and secure contents with a strip of cellophane tape. String the piñatas on a pole covered with crepe paper streamers and hang it just out of reach. Attach yarn to pole with tape so piñata will release when child pulls it.

"TREE OF LIFE"
Based on Mexican Christmas candelabrum, this "tree of life" is papier mâché. Sketch the tree shape on heavy wrapping paper, taped to plywood. Form a wire armature for the papier mâché. Soak one-inch newspaper strips in a creamy mixture of wallpaper paste and cold water. Squeezing out excess moisture, build up tree form. Keep back flat. Place tree in sun to dry. The figures are molded from papier mâché, and painted when dry with Mexican designs. Give entire tree two coats of gaudy yellow poster paint; designs are magenta. Set figures and star on toothpicks stuck into tree. Coat with clear shellac. Design by Beryl Foote.

Use paper cut-outs to decorate cans and greeting cards. Glue a strip of cardboard around rim of can to cover sharp edge. Fasten decorative drawer pull to lid top.

GIFT CONTAINERS

Stout oatmeal cartons or round ice cream containers can be decorated in a variety of ways to hold a king's treasure (junior version) of candy, small presents, or one bigger gift. Each box has its own liner, a removable drawstring bag of flannel, and is made to order as a container for sets of toys — tiny trains, tea sets, or wooden villages which are difficult for children to keep together.

The flannel bags are 7 by 17 inches. Fold a 16 by 18-inch rectangle in half; sew along two edges. In the hem at the top place a drawstring. When it is pulled, it becomes the tassel of the "cap."

Colored paper is pasted on and turned under at box ends. Faces may be either paper cutouts or marked on with poster paints. Trimmings are fringe, cotton, and black pressure-sensitive tape.

For decorations, cut out shapes you've drawn or traced on bright paper; rubber-cement them to package wrapping. Or you may use plastic paper with a sticky backing.

Make a fanciful figure for each child. Snowman is an oatmeal carton wrapped in cotton. Both the clown and Santa Claus are covered with pasted-on colored paper.

Covered cartons conceal surprises, like this animal emerging from clown's cap which is really a small cloth sack. Make the sack from flannel (see instructions).

KITCHEN CRAFTS

HOMEMADE CANDY GIFTS
How about a Christmas hobo pack to hold a gift of your homemade candies? Cover candy pieces in plastic wrap, place on a piece of cardboard, and then tie in a large square of nylon netting or costuming tarlatan. With a bright bow, tie the pack to a jumbo peppermint stick candy cane. Small versions of this idea, including only 3 or 4 pieces of candy, are nice favors for children who call during holidaytime, or for caroling groups.

FOR A YOUNG COOK
The youngest cook in the family will appreciate having her own book of recipes. This one has an added attraction—tucked inside are ingredients which she can use in trying out the recipes.

For the book, buy a small photograph album (the kind with the clear plastic pages designed as envelopes to hold snapshots). Select simple recipes and write them clearly on one side of file cards. Place each card in one of the album's envelopes. In the facing envelope put an ingredient sample. Good sample choices are flat packages of soft drink powder, soup mixes, gravy mix, powdered spaghetti sauce. Also include herbs measured out into squares of wax paper, folded and taped tight; and colored sugars to trim cakes and cookies.

Put in a packet of new cards to encourage the girl to add recipes. As a final touch tie a cluster of colored measuring spoons to the outside of the book.

SANTA CLAUS COOKY
Let Santa smile at the children from the kitchen wall while they enjoy their breakfasts on the exciting days before Christmas! Wrap a large frosted cooky in plastic film and attach it to a bread board on the wall. Decorate it with silver leaves, coconut, ornaments, and ribbon. (See page 27 for recipe and directions.)

Here's a surprise for a young hobo with a sweet tooth.

Recipe book "comes to life" with sample food packets.

Beaming face of Santa presides over the breakfast table.

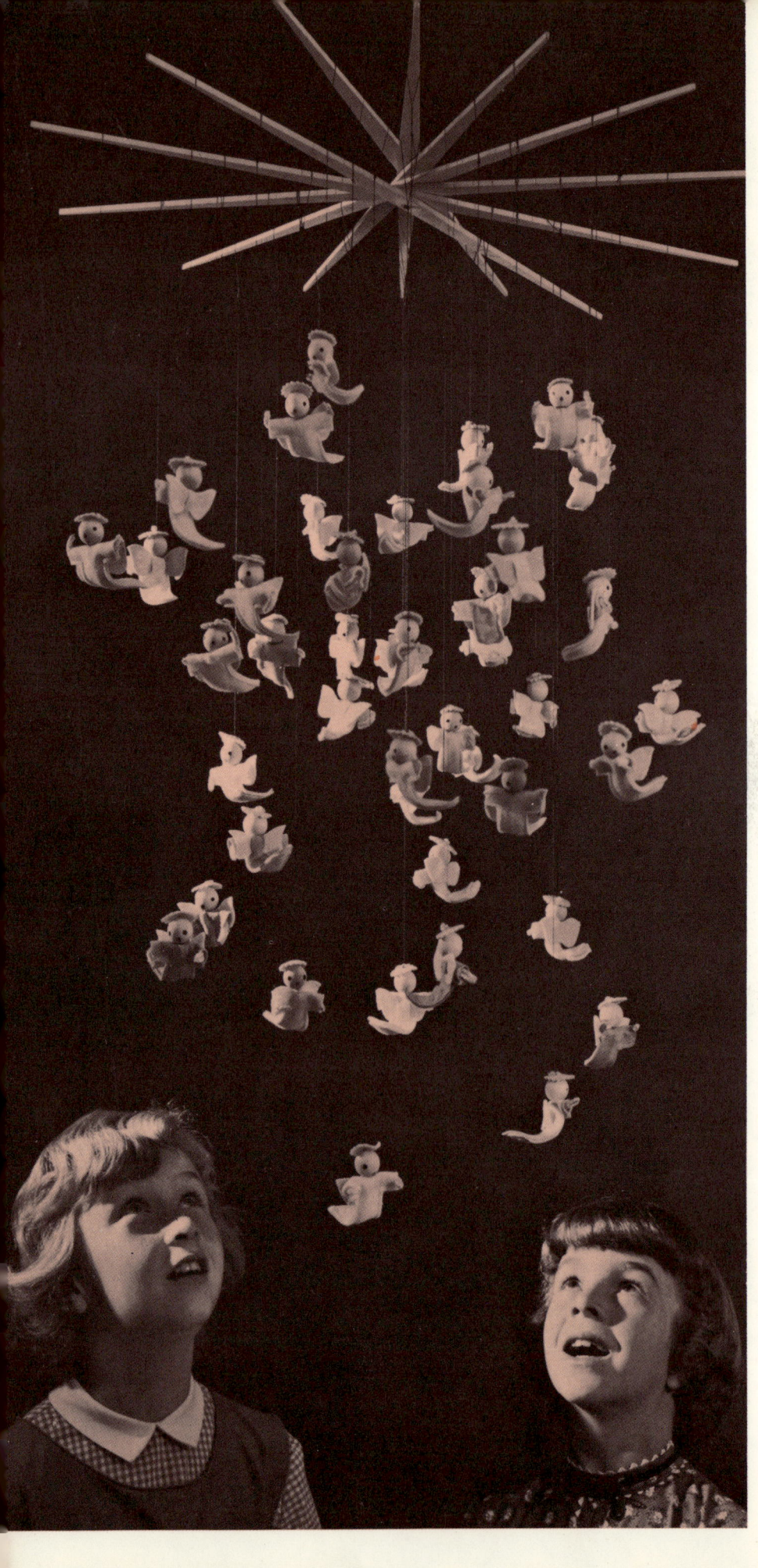

A CLOUD OF ANGELS HUNG FROM ABOVE

Perhaps your family has the friendly custom of giving small holiday callers homemade ornaments to take home.

At the end of a Christmas party suspended angels are ideal to pluck and give to departing children. Two or three also may be fastened to a fir branch and carried as a present to the children of a home you may be visiting during the holidays.

Materials you will need are: felt in several pastel shades, ¾-inch wooden beads, chenille pipe cleaners, model airplane dope, and black thread.

Angels in cloud are suspended with black threads of many different lengths from thin pieces of pine fastened together at centers and fanned out into multi-pointed star.

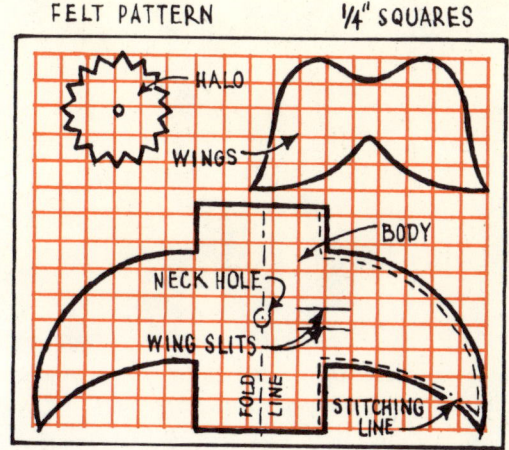

If you provide patterns, young hands will do the cutting. Each angel needs felt pieces: body, wings, and halo.

Stitching is job for grown-up. Dip matchstick in red and black airplane dope to add angel's eyes, mouth.

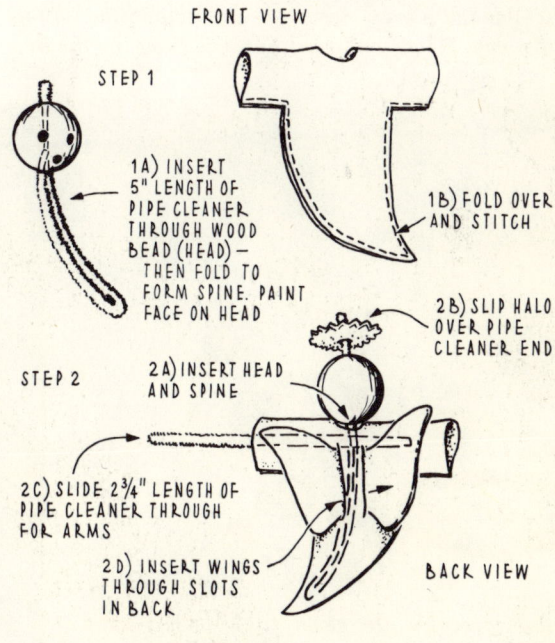

33

Children can decorate small felt tree with ornaments and pin up their Christmas cards. "Branches" are braid.

Gold-painted sardine cans make frames for felt figures. Assemble felt pieces, decorate, and glue to the bottom of the can. Heads are wood buttons. Hang by the bow.

Santa's features are glued to 14-inch cooky-filled candy jar. Hat comes off with the lid. Double thick felt should be used for arms and beard. Sequin eyes, bead nose.

FELT... VERSATILE AND EASY TO USE

Felt is one of the most versatile materials available for your Christmas projects. It has a more interesting texture than paper, plus some extra uses, and it is almost as easy to work with. Felt needs no hemming, may be zig-zagged with pinking shears and polka-dotted with a paper punch. It is available in bright colors and several weights. Felt can be glued as well as sewn.

These photographs are merely to *suggest* a number of ways you can create whimsical Christmas gifts and decorations of felt for the pleasure of your children. To make the stockings shown below, cut a paper pattern; trace twice around on felt. Measure around edge (except top) and cut an inch-wide strip for stocking thickness. Whipstitch with nylon thread for strength needed when presents swell the stockings out.

For other felt projects, see page 82 for a child's skirt; page 80, slippers; page 85, trimmings for sweaters; page 32, tiny angels for Christmas decorations.

Packages are tied with wide, bright ribbon and given a three-dimensional look with perky felt figures, multi-colored letters. For how to make stockings, see above.

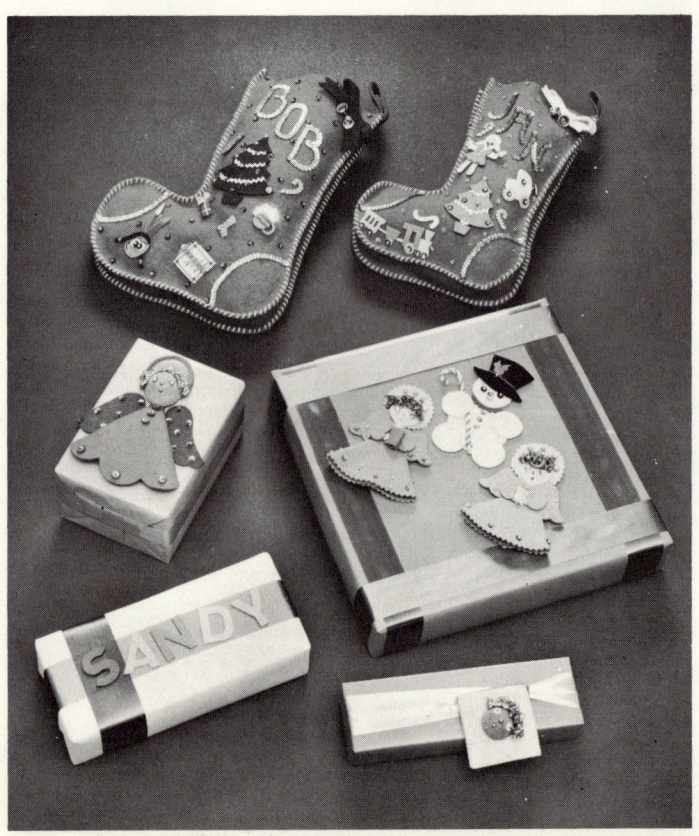

BEESWAX CANDLES AND COOKY TREES

Decorated cookies really show off on this Christmas tree bedecked with tinsel, shiny balls, chain of popcorn.

BEESWAX CANDLES
These honeycomb-textured candles not only are attractive but making them is fast and neat—fast enough to satisfy a child and neat enough to satisfy you.

The wax comes in thin 8 by 16¾-inch sheets with a honeycomb pattern. Buy it in various colors in hobby shops or from mail order houses under "Beekeeping equipment."

To make a candle, you merely place a piece of wicking on a beeswax sheet and roll it into a cylinder. Your candle is ready to use immediately. Wax rolls best at room temperature. Place sheet on smooth surface and cut the wicking slightly longer than width of beeswax. Place wick about ⅜ inch from one edge, press it down firmly to hold wick. Roll cylinder.

Because beeswax is slightly sticky, the depressions will catch glitter and sequins without adhesive. Scatter sequins on paper and roll finished candle over them.

COOKY TREE
The fun of making Christmas cookies is never outgrown by mothers and the results will always fascinate little children. To display the prettiest ones, hang them on a tree made of painted dowels. Use 1-inch dowel for trunk, drill holes at intervals to accept ¼-inch dowel branches. Glue in place.

Push trunk into clay for support. Cover clay with greenery and ornaments. Add Christmas balls and tinsel to finish decorating the tree. Be sure to place a pretty plateful of cookies nearby so children won't be tempted to nibble at the laden tree!

GUMDROP TREES
Like gaily colored hors d'oeuvres, gumdrops on toothpicks protrude temptingly from styrene foam Christmas trees (see photo below). Cut toothpicks in half, affix gumdrops, and cover the tree in rows for an orderly effect. For the trunk, stick a round pencil into a clay-filled pot.

To make a many-colored candle of beeswax, first roll a slender taper, then roll it in several butted-up pieces of beeswax (different colors).

Gumdrop trees bear sugarplums on toothpick twigs.

DOLLHOUSES

Dollhouse and garden invite group play. A small child can easily reach into the house, which is elevated only 1 foot. Table height (30 inches) would be more convenient for older children from 7 years. Plants include yew, spruce, juniper, azara, Mugho pine, succulents, choisya, osmanthus. Seedlings, rooted cuttings are also suitable.

PATIO...PLANTS...EVEN A POOL

Children and hobby gardeners alike will delight in this dollhouse with a miniature garden. The fun of planning and planting falls mainly to adults. But the garden is made for — and belongs to — the children, who are impressed that the plants are growing and the garden is "real."

A ¾-inch plywood base for the house is about 24 by 48 inches and provides the top terrace of the garden. Individual room-size floor pieces of ¼-inch plywood are mounted on the heavier base. Between the floor pieces of each room a ¼-inch groove is left so that the main dividing walls and the interior walls may be slipped in and glued for support. *Interior* walls do *not* follow the slope of the roof — they are uniformly 4 inches high. Braces for the removable plywood roof lock against the main dividing walls.

Doors and windows are painted on paper and glued

36

Probably no toy in a little girl's life means so much to her as a dollhouse. Here she is the queen, the sole ruler of her junior-sized palace. The dollhouses on these pages range from the frankly elaborate to the most unpretentious. All are capable of providing a child with hours of play — a stage for her growth of imagination.

- LANDSCAPED DOLLHOUSE: Planting, terracing, even a swimming pool.
- HEXAGONAL HOUSE: It revolves!
- FOLDAWAY MODEL: Grandma can keep it handy until a little girl comes calling.
- BOOKCASE DOLLHOUSES: Easy and fun.
- FURNITURE: How-to-make-it ideas.

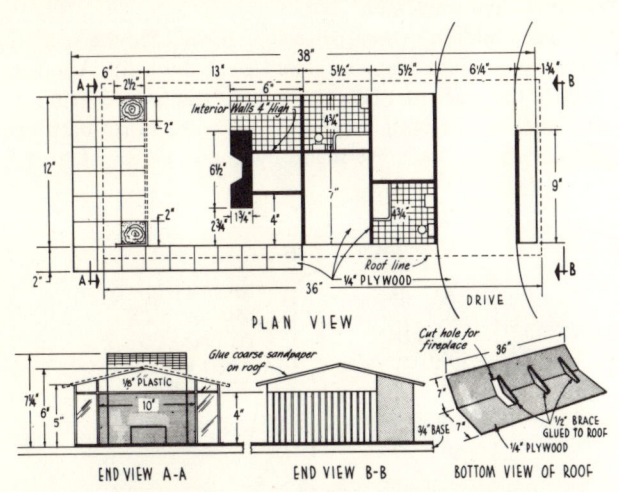

Interior walls, only 4 inches high, are glued to 3 main room dividers which slant up to center to support roof. One-eighth inch clear plastic is "glass" end wall.

Contemporary house is open on all sides so several children can play at one time. Or remove roof to see into all rooms. Photo was taken prior to landscaping.

to walls. Standard-size dollhouse furniture is used. The scale is about ½ inch to 1 foot.

The garden occupies a 4 by 6-foot box with a ¾-inch waterproof plywood bottom and 1 by 4-inch sides. Line box with tar paper and bore holes for drainage. The house, mounted on the 24 by 48-inch platform, rests on a 1 by 3-inch frame to keep it about the soil level. Use a light, porous soil mixture of 3 parts peat moss to 1 part soil. Patios and walks are mosaic tile. Edge the terrace with ¾-inch balsa wood and build a balsa fence. Brush cardboard with rubber cement and sprinkle with sand for driveway.

This English holly, like most plants here, is from a 3-inch pot. Restricted root space plus occasional pinching keeps plants small. Lawn is a flat of Irish moss.

Garden is on three levels. Pool (flower container) is set in insulating board. Dwarf spruce, succulents on second terrace. Notice paving of ¾-inch ceramic tiles.

Visiting child has fun rearranging furniture in this compact, ceiling-less, "foldaway" style dollhouse.

FOLDAWAY DOLLHOUSE

Children visitors often suffer from boredom because "there is nothing to do" while the adults chat. Grandmothers and aunts can easily make and furnish this folding dollhouse to keep handy when children come calling.

The house folds flat and packs into a 2 by 12 by 12-inch cardboard case when not in use. If you cover the case with attractive paper the entire dollhouse can be kept on a bookshelf. All the furniture goes into a small square box covered to match the house case.

To construct the house, join 8 pieces of cardboard. Cut four 1-foot-square pieces for floors of the four rooms. Four other cardboards, 9 by 12 inches, form the walls. Join these with gummed linen tape as shown in the plan right. When you tape the sections to each other, *be sure to leave adequate space* so that the house can fold up.

Furnishings and decorations can be quite inexpensive. Make as many as you wish and buy standard plastic pieces for the rest. Usually it is simpler to purchase the kitchen stove, refrigerator, and sink than it is to make them. However, other small pieces of furniture are fun to construct of balsa wood and scraps of fabric for upholstery.

For instance, the living room has a low bench and coffee table with thin balsa tops and slender balsa dowel legs glued in place. Tops are covered with adhesive plastic paper with simulated wood grain. The sofa has a wood frame padded slightly with cotton and covered with blue tweed cotton. Two-inch-square floor cushions are in bright colors of taffeta. Gold-backed paper with little holes punched in it and three 1-inch-high tiny dowels form a modern lamp. A large shiny black button with dollhouse-sized imitation flowers stuck in the holes becomes a floral arrangement for a table.

The children's room has a screen—cut from a section of bamboo place mat—to shield the baby crib. Another part of the place mat becomes a wide window covering in the kitchen. In both bedrooms, gathered skirts perk up plastic chairs. Beds are made by gluing pieces of heavy

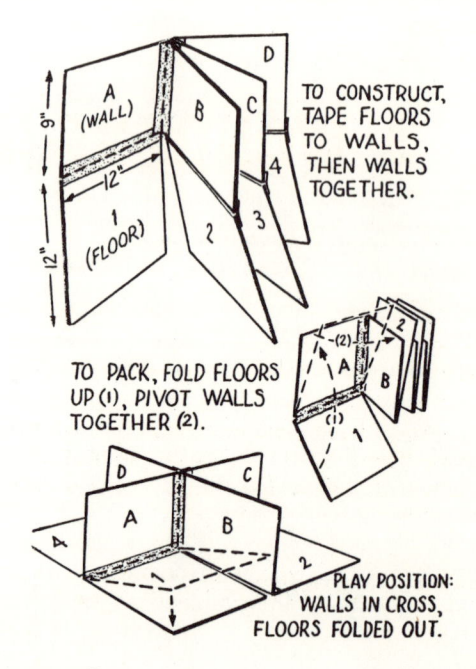

To construct house, join 8 pieces of cardboard with tape, allowing space between so the house will fold up.

cardboard together and padding them slightly before sewing on the full dust ruffles and coverlets.

Self-adhering plastic in various patterns is used throughout the house for wall coverings—wood grain for paneling the living room walls, floral for one bedroom, red-and-white striped for the children's room, plain pink for the kitchen. Confetti dot plastic becomes a floor covering in both bedroom and kitchen. A white wash cloth just fits the other bedroom for a luxurious rug and the living room floor is covered with glued-down red felt.

38

You cannot buy this delightful dollhouse anywhere, but you can build it yourself quite easily. It fits a card table or coffee table or sits on the floor. It would also be fine for the bedside of an invalid child.

A WONDERFUL DOLLHOUSE THAT REVOLVES

This dollhouse design is a rarity—one of the few that will allow two or more children to play without getting in each other's way. Each little room is a stage—open, wide, imaginative—and the house revolves smoothly on ball bearings. Small hands can pass things through the oversize doors. There is also an inside patio. The scale is ¾ inch to 1 foot, matching that of the most obtainable size of doll furniture. You may also make furniture from scraps of soft wood.

To lay out the floor, drive two brads through a yardstick 18 inches apart, for a compass. Draw the 36-inch circle, then arcs on its circumference to divide into six equal parts. Then draw in the room lines.

(continued on next page)

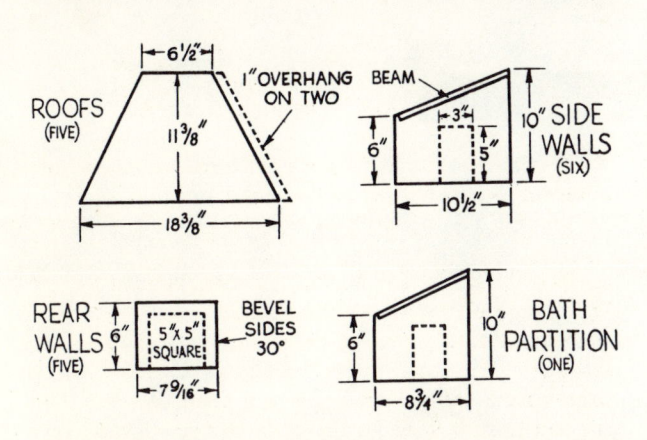

All lumber is cut from one 4 by 8-foot panel of ¼-inch fir plywood. You also need 2-foot circle of hardboard for base. Nail roof sections to the side wall beams.

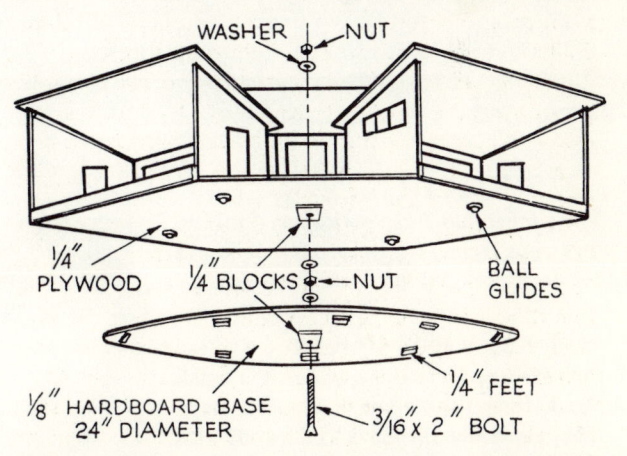

House revolves on base on four small ball furniture glides (single rolling ball bearing). Space them equidistant on 22-inch circle on underside of floor.

39

DOLLHOUSE (CONTINUED)

Assemble the house with white glue and small wire nails. Rear walls are beveled on sides to butt flat against side walls. This house is painted the same overall. While still wet, the roof was sprinkled with coarse silver glitter to simulate gravel.

1 · MASTER BEDROOM
You can also furnish the master bedroom as a family room. Furniture is homemade. Notice the king-size bed.

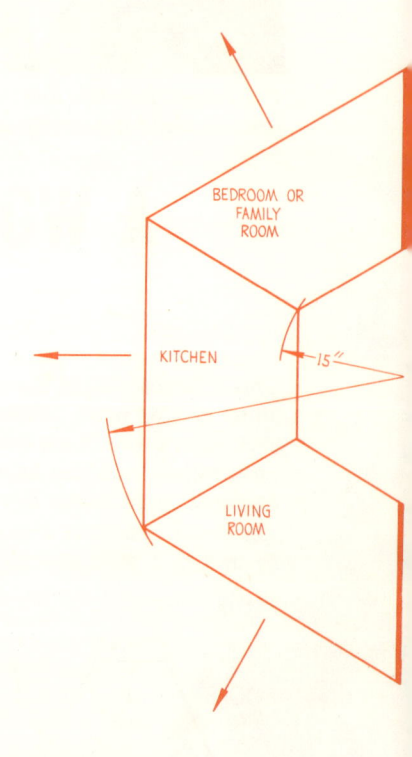

2 · KITCHEN
The kitchen has three doorways. Furnishings came from a toy store. All rooms have 1¼-inch plywood strip across outer edge.

3 · LIVING ROOM
Fireplace hood in living room is a small plastic funnel and a 1-inch diameter metal tube, glued together and to the roof with epoxy cement. Fire pit is a telescoping drinking cup. All are painted black. The furniture was jig-sawed from a 2-inch-thick piece of balsa wood.

4 · BATH AND LAUNDRY
The extra partition wall separates the bath from the laundry room. Bath fixtures were purchased; those of the laundry were cut from balsa wood and spray painted. Cabinet doors were outlined with pencil.

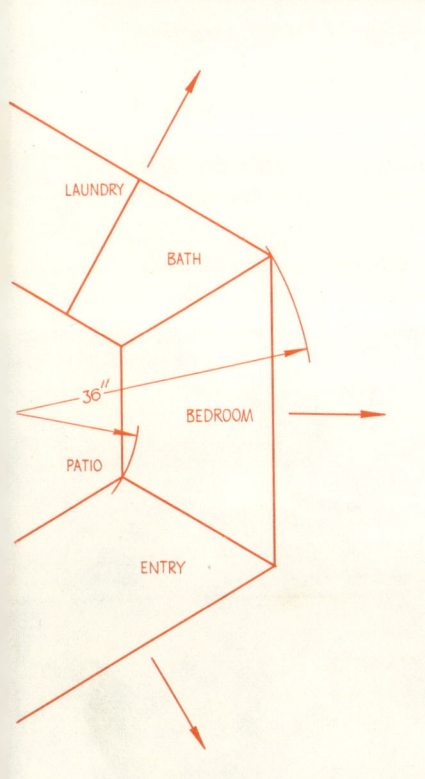

5 · BEDROOM
Furniture in this bedroom was purchased. A scrap of felt makes a rug. Mirror (from a purse) is glued to wall.

6 · ENTRY, PATIO
Entrance garden and patio floor were first painted brick-red. Then a grass mat and rubber shrubs (from a hobby shop) were glued in place. The trunk of the small tree in the middle of the patio is the axle bolt from the house's base. Its planter is a lid from a spray paint can.

A DOLL CAN LIVE IN A BOOKCASE...OR EVEN IN A STACK OF BOXES

Big advantage of boxes: versatility.

Small-scale play boxes and bookcases make excellent living quarters for a little girl's dolls. The six-room dollhouse pictured above sits on a bureau. The boxes are ⅜-inch plywood both nailed and glued. Each box is 8 by 8 by 12 inches. The boxes may be combined in many ways.

The little girl at the right now uses most of her bookcase for a doll apartment, but in several years, when she has outgrown dolls, the shelves could house a phonograph or hobby collection. This kind of cupboard costs about $15 unfinished. Or you can adapt any low bookcase.

DOLL FURNITURE

Furniture for the bookcase dollhouse isn't hard to make if you use balsa wood. Cut pieces with a single-edged razor. Enough balsa to make the furniture below costs about $1 at hobby shops.

Here's one caution: Thin balsa breaks easily, especially when unpainted. This furniture can take child-wear because it's braced, pinned, and glued. Pieces can be painted with spray-on paints from small-size pressure cans. Rugs of cloth scraps and pictures and windows of paper are added.

One room might be a miniature of the little girl's own room. Or let her decorate a room to suit a foreign doll.

Bookcase shelves make highly satisfactory room for dolls. Fireplace, windows, and pictures are glued to walls.

42

DOLLHOUSE WITH DOORS

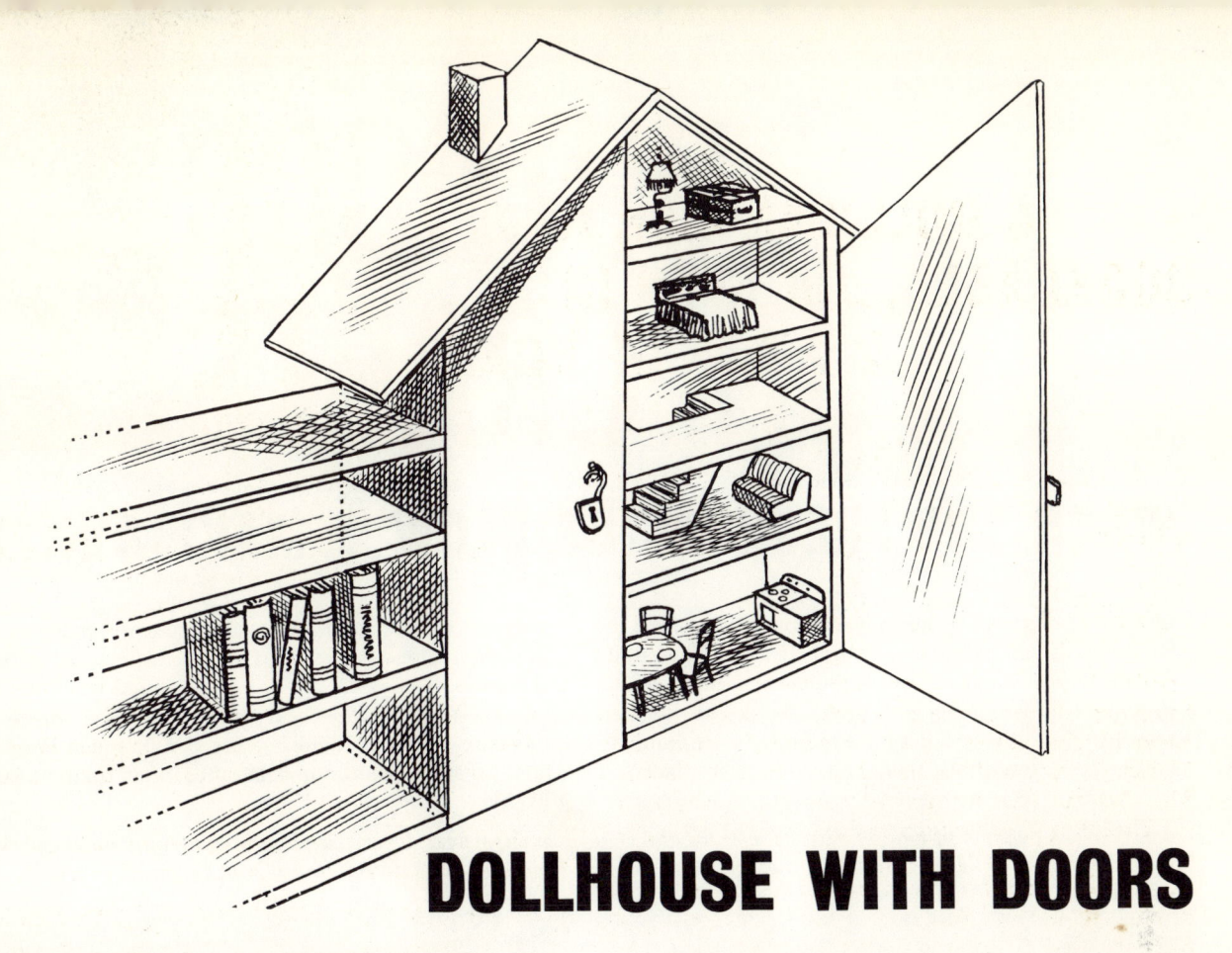

Father need not be an accomplished workshop whiz to produce a dollhouse such as this one. Basically, it is a bookcase—an old, discarded one or an inexpensive new one without the finish. Or you may prefer to build a simple bookcase yourself, using 1 by 10-inch lumber; if so, allow 12 inches height for the shelves to accommodate the many tall books that children like so well.

Doors and roof can be cut from ¼-inch plywood. Allow a generous overhang for the roof, at the front as well as on the sides. Doors must fall an inch or so short of a snug fit against the roof when they are closed, in order to permit clearance of the overhang.

Staircases between floors can be cut with an ordinary hand saw, although a power saw will do the job in less time. A leftover block of wood, painted bright red, makes an effective chimney and gives the house a touch of gaiety even when it is closed and locked.

Stores that sell paint and wallpaper may be able to supply you with extra scraps of wall covering or out-of-date sample books to use in decorating the walls. Remember that wallpaper which may seem too "busy" to suit your tastes may be ideal when reduced to the small-scale world of a doll's room.

Being able to lock up a dollhouse when it is not in use means fewer "tense moments" for parents to cope with. Baby brother (or big brother) will be forced to keep hands off, and whenever the young lady of the house resumes her dollhouse activities she will find everything as she left it.

There is a less obvious—but equally important—advantage in having doors such as the ones shown here: When the doors are swung outward to enclose her on both sides, a little girl feels as though she is actually *living* in the tiny rooms. Outside activity is shut off from her peripheral vision, and the vicarious joys of dollhouse play can be enjoyed to the fullest.

In later years, when doll furniture has been carefully packed away and the house's proud owner has grown up, the house can continue to serve a useful purpose as storage space in the workshop or garage.

OUTDOOR FUN CRAFTS

WHEN THE FRESH WINDS BLOW...MAKE A KITE!

Kite flying seems to be enjoying a revival as a pastime the entire family can delight in — adults help the children build and paint the kite, and *all* join in the fun of seeing it go up. Families who like flying kites give these as some of their reasons: You usually don't have to go far from home to find a good launching spot; and kites offer plenty of variety, for wind conditions vary enough to make even a perfectly balanced kite fly in a different way each time it is sent up.

Although the diamond-shaped two- and three-stick kites are the most familiar, they can be made in nearly any form. Oriental models often look like birds or

The ancient pastime of kite flying puts modern children into the realm of jet flight. Lives there a boy — or a man — who doesn't send part of himself up there as he watches his kite ride the wind skyward?

Children have a special rapport with the outdoors and all things related — carrying home driftwood or shells prolongs their original adventure, wind-strewn kites thrill them, a small plant in a bowl brings the outdoors inside.
- **KITES**: Fundamentals — plus some variations — on the ancient craft of kite-making.
- **BIRD FEEDERS** — and a bird bath made from a coconut cut in two.
- **TINY BOWL GARDENS**: A convalescent child loves these "souvenirs from outdoors."
- **GOURDS**: Whimsical and versatile.
- **CATCHING FISH** — plaster ones, that is.
- **GAMES** to take traveling, other ideas...

dragons. It takes several men to launch and fly a kind called the centipede, which is made of 25 separate discs that stretch 40 feet when the kite is aloft!

FLYING FACTORS
Of course, specific factors decide whether any kite will fly well or barely get off the ground. The most obvious of these is weight. A kite's weight should be as low as possible in relation to its surface area, with this qualification — the covering material and framing sticks must be strong enough to withstand the force of the wind. In general, good kite-flying winds have a velocity of 10 to 15 miles per hour.

MAKING THE KITE
Here's a refresher course in how kites go together. Most of them have two main parts: a frame that holds it rigid, and a light covering over the frame that catches the wind. The operator controls the kite with a line from kite to a bridle that holds kite angled to the wind.

Kites may be flat or bowed — the shape often affects the way they fly. Basswood, clear white pine, and spruce are used for frames. Balsa is usually not strong enough. If the kite frame does not support every area of the cover, a strong wind will distort it.

Cover the frame with tissue or a closely-woven fabric like cambric or nylon. The stronger the wind, the heavier the covering should be.

TAILS AND BRIDLES
A flat kite needs a long tail to get enough wind resistance to hold it up. Unless the wind is unusually strong, tails aren't needed on most box or bowed kites. Use strips of cloth, tissue paper, or plastic film. Tie strips in bow-ties every 12 inches on a length of string. Except for tiny kites, you'll need at least a 15-foot tail.

Make a bridle of several threads fastened to different parts of the frame. Join them to the top part because their job is to keep the kite headed into the wind. A bowed kite needs at least two strings; a flat kite, three. Each leg of the bridle should be half the length of the cross-stick. For a line, wrap several hundred feet of string on a reel that will let you unwind the twine easily.

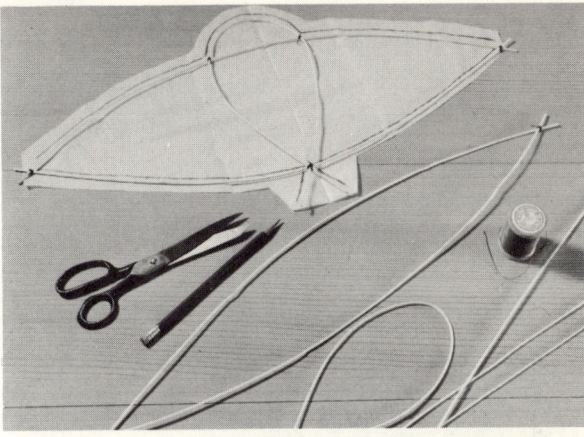

1. Dampen bamboo strips for flexibility. Carefully bend and tie securely to form hawk kite frame. Trace frame on tissue; cut paper slightly larger than outline.

2. Fold edges of tissue paper over bamboo carefully; paste it in place. Note that wing tips are not covered. Paint flying hawk design on side away from frame.

3. Tie thread between wing tips for bow shape. Add a 3-leg bridle to convex side; one leg tied to each top wing piece, third to where tail pieces meet. Add cloth tail.

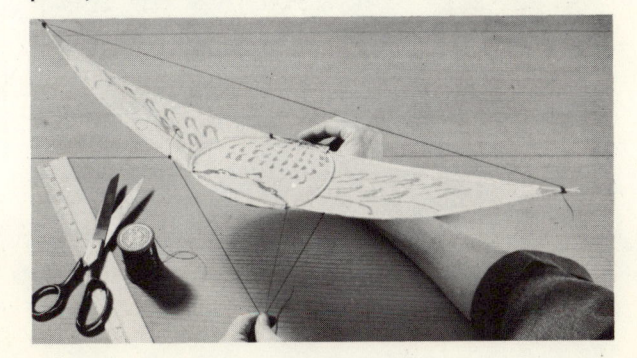

HOW TO MAKE A THREE-STICK KITE

Satisfying flying can be had from a standard three-stick kite. And often it's a good idea to build a simple kite like this before trying a complicated one. You can vary the size of the kite as long as the proportions stay the same.

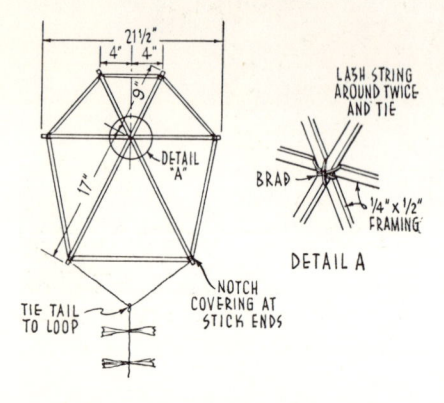

Cut the framing pieces with a knife. Put them in position and wrap the center joint with strong twine. Notch both ends of each framing piece and stretch twine between the notches to outline the kite's shape.

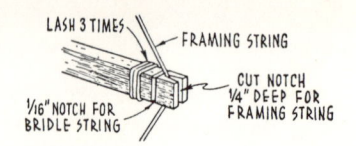

To keep wood from splitting, wrap stick ends tightly with string.

Lay frame on top of covering material and cut out the cover; leave 2 inches to spare all around. You may decorate the cover with oils and poster paint. Now fold the cover over the framing twine. Glue or stitch it in place so the cover is firm but not tight.

You can fly a three-stick kite either flat or bowed. If you want your kite flat, add about 20 feet of tail, as shown in the sketch at left. A tail that is light and bulky works better than a narrow, heavy one. Wrap the tail around a piece of cardboard when you're not flying the kite.

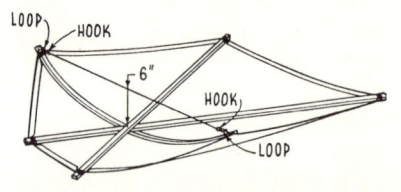

If you are making a bowed kite, fasten a length of twine between the two ends of the horizontal crosspiece. Fasten the ends of the twine into loops at the ends of the crosspiece.

JAPANESE KITES

Kite-making is a cultural gift of the Orient. Vividly colored Japanese kites below, made of rice paper and bamboo, are available in Oriental shops. Six-foot carp in center acts like a windsock, doesn't really fly.

WHY DOES A KITE FLY?

While you and your children are making the kite, or, at the latest, when it is finally airborne, you will get the question: "Why does a kite fly?" Why does it go up, then soar and climb after it's in the air? There *are* complicated aerodynamic formulas, but here is a simpler explanation.

The kite string holds the kite headed into the wind at approximately a 45° angle. Air blowing against the kite's surface gets redirected and forms a push on the underside of the kite and a partial vacuum above it (see sketch).

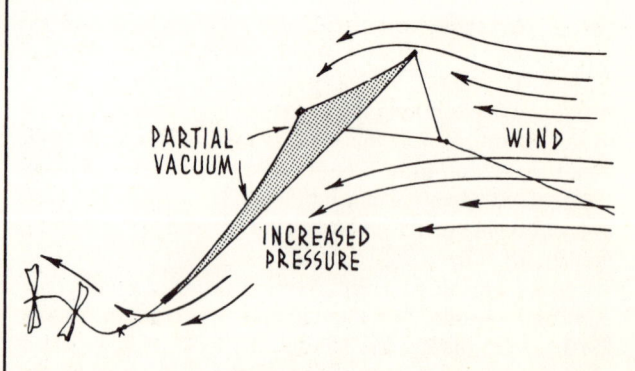

Both of these pressures tend to force the kite up. If the pressures are stronger than the downward weight of the kite, tail, and line, the kite will rise and soar.

Saw a coconut in half, or remove a quarter of it. Don't take out the meat — birds will enjoy a tropical feast.

Above: Wire on each side provides extra perches. Right: Birds can stand on rim. Hang from wires to keep away from cats.

MAKE FRIENDS WITH THE BIRDS

Bird bath: Cut the top third from coconut shell; remove meat. Follow above drawing for looping twine holder.

COCONUT CUP OR FEEDER
Observing birds feeding in the yard is one of the earliest and most pleasant contacts with nature a child can have. Coconut shells are simple but effective means of encouraging birds.

PINE CONE FEEDER
Most families enjoy a bird feeding station, especially in climates where winter food is scarce. Here's one that's easy to prepare. The base is a pine cone. For the food, melt some unsalted fat, mix in a bit of cornmeal or bird seed. With the cone tip up, pour the warm mixture into packets between its scales. When the fat hardens, feeder is ready for use. When children make their own bird cone feeders, give them small pieces of suet to push between the scales.

SAFE FROM MARAUDERS
Keeping squirrels and chipmunks from robbing the birds is often as great a problem as marauding cats. Here is a feeder built to avoid both hazards. An inverted 10-pound tin is painted and fastened below a feeding tray. It is supported by a 5-foot length of 2-inch pipe set about a foot in the ground. A little roof keeps the food dry. Tray is far enough away from trees to keep cats from jumping onto the feeder. And the pipe and inverted can discourage climbing cats and squirrels.

Length of pipe topped by an inverted tin can keeps food safe from cats, squirrels, chipmunks.

Suet-filled pine cone tempts hungry birds. It is attractive enough to be hung near the house where birds can best be seen. Cone is secured with wire.

Ten-inch-high Pieris japonica is a miniature tree around which a whimsical wooden vagabond strolls nonchalantly. Rosettes of Saxifraga umbrosa primuloides outline white gravel road. Pieris root ball is packed firmly with moist peat moss.

Most of the year, a youngster lives and plays in an outdoor world of flowers, shrubs, and trees. When the confinement of cold weather comes, a bit of the outdoors brought inside is a pleasant surprise. Each of these miniature gardens can be an adventure for children—a small plant in a small container is just about irresistible.

Plants for these little gardens should be chosen on the basis of temporary compatibility to the indoors. They should be kept in fairly cool rooms and watered carefully. Later, in the springtime or perhaps for a family Arbor Day event, the little plant is set out as the child's own contribution to the family outdoor garden.

When looking for containers, don't limit yourself necessarily to those intended only for plants. Many small casseroles, trays, baking dishes, or bowls for fruit are usable for miniature gardens.

Prepare the planter in this way: Make a mixture of one-third soil, one-third peat moss, and one-third sand. Except in very shallow containers, place an inch of small pebbles or charcoal over the entire bottom to act as a soil sweetener, as there are no drain holes. There are also commercial potting mixtures available. These must be made very damp before using as they contain perlite and peat moss. A plant in this mixture must be kept constantly moist.

A BIT OF OUTDOORS...BROUGHT INSIDE

White deer (candles) give peat moss-banked azalea a woodland touch. Azaleas should be kept cool and set out in the garden soon.

Six-inch pine was planted in bonsai pot as a 3-inch seedling 3 years ago.

Plants in shallow pan are carrot, beet, turnip tops which have been planted in vermiculite for a month.

FOR FANCY FOLIAGE...
PLANT ROOT VEGETABLES

Here's an old trick, but still a good one. Show children how to start an indoor garden with root vegetables from your kitchen. Grow them in a bowl just deep enough to hold an inch of water and some pebbles to anchor them down. Or grow them in pots filled with a mixture of sand and peat moss. To nourish these gardens as you keep them moist, put a teaspoon of nitrogen-rich commercial fertilizer in each quart of water used.

• *Carrots, parsnips, turnips, beets.* The top inch of any of these will throw up several luxuriant stems of new leaves. Carrots produce lacy green plumes of foliage, and the beets show ruffled rosettes of puckered leaves in bronzes and reds touched with purple. Both parsnips and turnips have toothed, hairy foliage flaring out in strong curves.

• *Hanging baskets.* Hollow out any of the four vegetables above with an apple corer so you can keep water in their hollow cups, and grow them as hanging baskets. Hang singly or tie several together with raffia. Shortly after you hang them, leaves grow from the tips of the roots and begin to curl upward, eventually hiding the roots. You may have to add water several times a day. Never let them dry out.

• *Old-timers.* Grown in water, both sweet potatoes and yams produce luxuriant vines with shiny, crisp, heart-shaped leaves. Yam leaves are green with russet touches. Grow these in a tall hyacinth vase filled with water. Or, grow them in a narrow bowl, holding the tuber itself above the water so that only the root end is wet. As the vine stems lengthen, give them support and let them climb.

Foil-covered carton contains jade plant, sedum, hen-and-chickens. Notice the mulch of white pebbles.

TINY SUCCULENT GARDENS

Especially to sick youngsters, these tiny succulent gardens are attractive. They are wonderful substitutes for bedside bouquets — easy to arrange, easy to care for. The child can decorate them with little paper favors.

The neat little containers are small cottage cheese cartons covered with gold foil. The top of each carton, also foil-covered, serves as the saucer needed for the occasional watering.

Cuttings and subdivisions of succulents, mostly the smaller kinds, are planted in sandy soil. Among those used here are crassula, echeveria, graptopetalum, hen-and-chickens, and sedum. Add little paper decorations hung by thread from tiny bamboo sticks.

Child can be fancy-free in decorating these little planters with tissue paper favors available at party shops.

GOURDS...
THE TOYS YOU CAN GROW IN YOUR GARDEN

Whimsical woodpecker's bill is a small gourd glued to a long, dumbbell-shaped gourd. Gourd hanging from top of page at left is a curtain pull.

Here's a mallard duck to float in a child's pool. Small gourd (head) is glued to large gourd (body). Seal with varnish after the duck is painted.

Small gourds are ideal toys for little children. Light and durable, they rattle when shaken. After you clean and dry them, paint bright-colored designs.

Gourds seem to be made to order for children's gardens—they are fairly easy to grow, can take the huge amounts of water youngsters like to give, and have marvelous fruit to watch develop!

In the spring, plant 3 or 4 seeds about an inch deep in fertilized hills four feet apart. Later, thin to 2 plants. They grow rapidly and require much water. No two vines seem to produce exactly the same results—you'll get many colors, many shapes from a packet of seeds. Harvest the fruit after the frost and before the winter rains spoil them. Wax the gourds.

To keep them *permanently,* dry gourds thoroughly by hanging in a dry, well-ventilated place. After slow drying, soak them overnight in cold water or cover them with boiling water until waxy outer covering softens. Scrape this off with pen knife or paint will not adhere. Do any cutting of gourds while they are still damp. Use knife or keyhole saw.

They may be made water resistant by first smoothing with steel wool and then coating with hot paraffin. Dry them for a few days; then paint. Treat surface like wood surface: sandpaper lightly, do any gluing with wood glue. Although any wood paint is good, poster paint is especially effective. Apply a durable coat of shellac or spar varnish. You may also burn designs with a wood-burning needle.

50

1. With hands, scoop out in wet sand a shape about 6 by 12 inches, not over 2 inches deep.

2. For decoration press shells, rocks, marbles into bottom of mold. Poke holes with fingers.

3. Fill large coffee can two-thirds full of water, add plaster until it mounds above water.

4. Pour less-detailed sections of mold first to keep everything in place. Then pour all at once.

water will absorb it. Stop when the plaster begins to form a mound above the water. Let it stand for 2 minutes, then stir the mixture carefully from the bottom, blending in as little air as possible. You can use your hand, a stick, or an old spoon. Stir for a minute, wait 3 minutes, and then pour.

If you want to hang up the piece when it's finished, push eye-bolts or twisted wire about halfway into the casting. Or decorate the top with more shells if both sides will show.

Do this immediately because the plaster starts to heat up and harden at once. Then wash the plaster off your hands and clean any tools which you plan to use again. Plaster is hard to remove after it has set.

Let plaster harden in mold for half an hour; then loosen the sand around edges of the molded piece. Carefully lift it out. Wash off the finished product and scrape away excess sand. If you like, paint the form with poster paints after it dries.

You can also do this project in the back yard with about two sacks of sand, poured into a box and then moistened.

SAND CASTING AT THE BEACH...OR IN YOUR BACK YARD

There's more than one way to catch fish at the ocean! Forms below were cast in beach sand with plaster.

A beach trip would be an ideal time and place for children to cast a simple plaster of Paris form to be used as a wall plaque or a decorative garden piece. Everything they need is at the beach except the plaster itself.

You will need about 5 pounds of plaster for a form like those shown here. Choose a moist spot just below the high water level, where the tide won't cover your mold before it is finished. Scoop out a simple shape about 2 inches deep. When you place ornamental beach rocks, shells, marbles, or bits of tiles from home in the bottom of the mold, be sure to push them into the sand less than halfway so they will be firmly embedded in the plaster.

Mix plaster in a coffee can. Add plaster as long as the

"QUIET-TIME" CRAFTS FOR CAMPING VACATIONS

When you're planning what to take along on a camping vacation, you may want to include some of this simple equipment for the "quiet time" activities—the short periods when the children stop climbing trees and rocks to catch their breath.

STAMP PRINTS
You can print objects like shells, eucalyptus pods, and

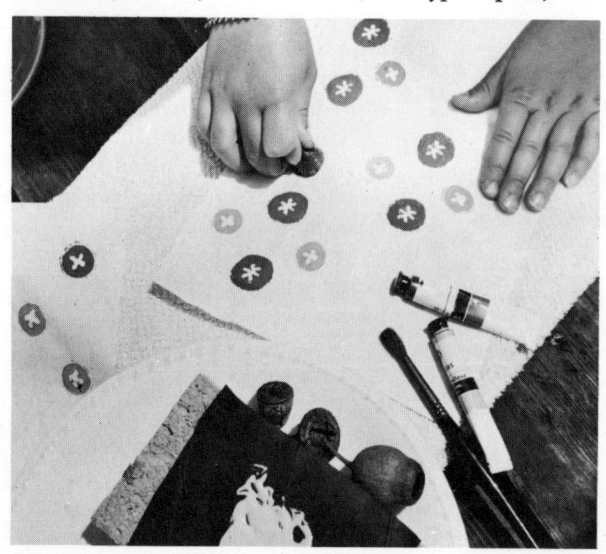

To make paper place mats, press flat side of eucalyptus pod into ink on paint pad; then press on paper.

pine cone scales by stamping them directly onto paper. You need a minimum of materials: water-base paint, a small square of old inner tube for a pad, and paper (a roll of paper towels or shelf paper is fine). Do your printing on something that "gives"—a pile of newspapers or a folded towel.

For a good print, the pod should have one fairly flat surface. Trim with a knife to increase the area that will contact the paper. Pour a small amount of paint onto the tubing and press the pod you want to print into it. Then stamp on paper in any arrangement you choose.

The stamping technique is so easy you'll probably want to experiment with various patterns, possibly drawing in backgrounds. Use stamp prints to decorate stationery, book covers, paper placemats. For permanency, spray with clear plastic.

SPRAY OR SPATTER PRINTS
If you want to make pleasing prints with an absolute minimum of effort, take along several pressurized spray cans of paint. This paint has an oil base and won't be affected if you get water on the prints.

Older girls would like this project. Since the paint can be used on fabrics, they might like to take along some plain yardage so that they can print skirt material or a pair of curtains for their room at home as a souvenir of their camping trip. (Wash fabric first at home to remove sizing.) Use unbleached muslin, sheeting, Indian head, or osnaburg. Select evergreen boughs, fern leaves, or large wildflowers—natural materials that have a strong, somewhat irregular form. Hold the paint can about a foot away from the fabric; spray lightly for a spattered effect, more heavily for a darker background color. Since the natural materials act as stencils, the paint will outline their shapes on the fabric.

Even smaller children can have fun making leaf prints by spatter painting. Carefully pin leaves (large, bold spe-

Place fern leaves on paper or fabric; spray with pressurized paint can. Mask the area you don't want sprayed.

cimens are best) to the paper. Place pins with heads *inside* the shape of the leaf so you won't get a pin design on your print, too! Dip a discarded toothbrush into colored ink or water paint. Then, holding it over the surface to be printed, draw a flat stick or piece of cardboard *toward you* across the toothbrush. When the leaf is removed from the paper, an attractive silhouette will be left behind. Interesting effects are obtained by shading off toward the edges and by using different colors of paper, paint, and ink.

PRESERVING FLOWERS BY DRYING IN SUN, SAND

Preserving wildflowers and autumn leaves is an activity that both young and old can enjoy. Probably everyone is familiar with the procedure of pressing flowers between the pages of a book. A comic book or other publication made of absorbent paper is best. Weight book down so flowers will dry to paper thinness. Shift flowers during drying period so that their moisture won't cause them to mold.

Drying flowers in their natural shape takes a bit more skill. This method is preferable: Place a layer of fine, warm sand on the bottom of a paper box. Lay several flowers on top of the sand, face up; gently sift the sand between petals until flower is covered. It takes about 18 days to dry them at room temperature (or, in a 100° to 125° oven, 12 to 24 hours). When flowers are dry, cut hole in bottom corner of box to release sand. Sand-dried flowers retain both their natural shape and color.

WAXING FRESH FLOWERS

You may also preserve wildflowers in paraffin. Use 2 or 3 pounds—it is reusable. Take a tall juice can and shave paraffin into it. Place the container in a pan of water and melt paraffin over the stove. (Do not place the container directly on the flame as you may start a fire—paraffin is flammable!) As soon as wax is melted and cooled to lukewarm, dip the flower in the liquid. Hold the stem with the flower down and swish it around once or twice. Quickly but gently shake off excess wax. Turn upright and let wax set a few minutes. Then immerse flower in cold water to harden; or, clip it upside-down on a line. When dry, the flower in its transparent paraffin coating will look waxy. Autumn colored foliage preserved this way is particularly attractive.

FISH PRINTS

Let your son make a lasting record of the fish he caught on vacation—the one that didn't get away! It will be a decorative print to frame and display. Supplies are easy to take along in the car or boat: cardboard from grocery carton, straight pins, India ink (pack it and handle it carefully—remember that it is indelible), medium paint brush, spray can of fixative, several sheets of rice paper. The last three materials are available at art supply stores.

Lay fish on cardboard; fix fins and tail with pins. Spray with fixative to seal the pores and let dry. Then paint fish quickly with India ink. Smooth away any trapped ink from the crevices to prevent blotting. Center a piece of rice paper over inked fish, lay it on lightly, and press gently but firmly from tail forward to make imprint. Peel off paper and you'll see a black-and-white print which reveals the intricate scale pattern. Let it dry and then mount.

Preserve flowers by dipping in slightly cooled paraffin. Camellia shown here, but method also works with wildflowers. Melt wax in double boiler, or can in pan of water.

Fish prints, mounted on hardboard and framed with mat and glass, provide lasting record of your son's vacation.

Pin fish (perhaps from local fish market) to cardboard. Spray with fixative; paint with India ink to seal.

Here is a cat in a bamboo "goldfish bowl" surrounded by citizens of the sea. Fanciful driftwood fish mobiles, suspended from a family room ceiling beam, evolved from pieces that were gathered along the beach.

DRIFTWOOD MOBILES

The driftwood you and your children pick up along the beach can be turned into whimsical fish mobiles. It does not take much to get started—a few simple tools, including a pen knife, clothespins for clamps, white glue, wire, screw eyes and swivels, plus the pieces of driftwood or water-beaten cork or bark.

You may prefer to start with a piece of bark because it's soft and easier to work with. Bring out the fish form by whittling and carving the wood. Attach eyes of sequins, marbles, buttons, or small shells, with white glue. You may wish to turn a shape on the lathe or do some joinery to add a three-dimensional fin or tail.

After making a few forms, attach screw eyes and swivels and hang mobiles from varied lengths of wire. Your collection of driftwood "marine life" could grow to include a sea gull, a turtle, or a crab.

These pieces suggest fish forms. The shapes are to be delineated with a pen knife.

Tools include knife, saw, rasp, clothespin clamps, glue, wire, screw eyes and swivels, whetstone, and oil.

SOUVENIR PANEL

What family doesn't return from a trip laden with a miscellany of souvenirs they can't bear to throw away? By fixing these on a panel for den or family room, you can keep vacation memories warm for your children. Your family's tastes for your own "travel wall" will dictate the results.

Pictorial souvenirs help to establish the overall design. Use maps, posters, post cards, photographs, menu covers, stamps, luggage stickers and windshield stickers. Travel documents help to make the record personal. From foreign travels, especially, it's fun to keep such things as tourist cards, passport photos, paper money, and receipts.

For the backing use hardboard, thin plywood, or heavy cardboard. Wallpaper paste works well on large paper areas such as travel posters. Be sure to brush it on evenly to avoid air bubbles. Household adhesives are easier to handle on small items. White glue works well on three-dimensional objects—a straw hat, pine cone, shells, coins. Finally, give a protective coating of spray-on plastic.

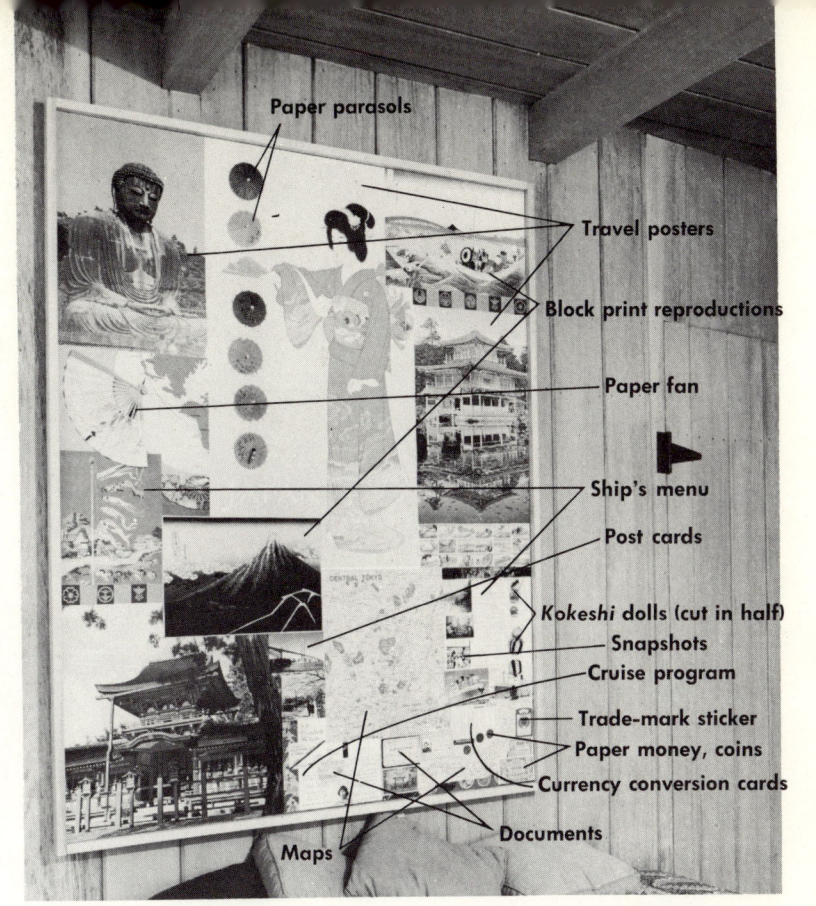

Wall panel is interesting record of a cruise to Japan. Route is marked on maps. Panel is 4 by 5 feet, displays money, souvenirs.

TWO UNIQUE DISPLAY BOARDS

Simple but handsome display board is created from a 10-year-old boy's collection of shells.

NATURE COLLECTIONS

A display board will inspire any youngster to do something with his shells, pine cones, or other small trophies from the outdoors. Provide these materials for one good way of making a nature exhibit: cardboard, a frame, sand, white glue, and epoxy glue (a type of household cement which has great holding powers). First, cut cardboard to fit frame; paint cardboard with white glue and sift a lot of sand on it. When dry, shake off excess sand.

Wait one day and arrange shells or rocks in a pleasing design next to the frame. One-by-one, glue objects on the sand-covered surface by using one of the strong epoxy glues. On the back of the frame, each shell is labeled with its proper name and where it was located.

55

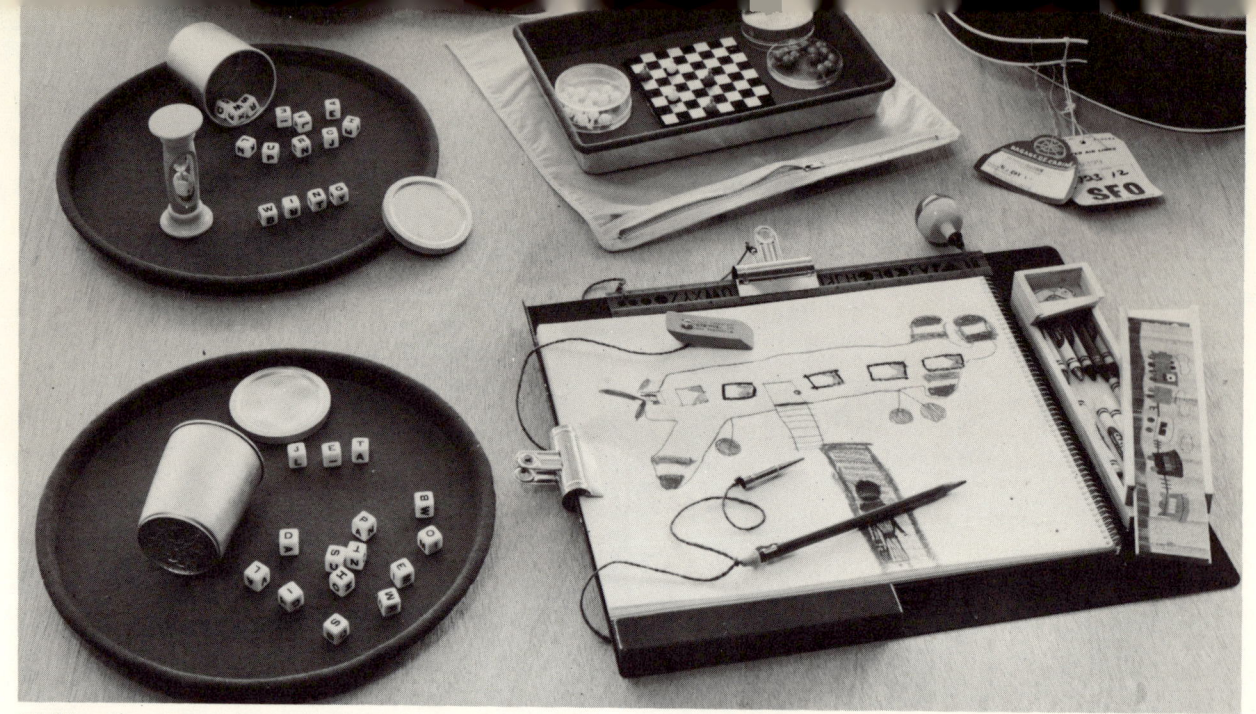

Children are better travelers if they can occupy themselves. Games are better travelers if modified for on-the-move playing. Tie or clamp loose equipment; use felt-covered pans for tables. Pack games in separate bags.

THESE GAMES ARE GOOD TRAVELERS

Good travel games can charm youngsters into being remarkably good travelers. The main difficulty is to find *games* that are good travelers! To qualify, a game should involve equipment that stays intact, withstands wear, doesn't raise too much noise, and does not require more space than the confines of a seat in a train, plane, bus, or automobile.

There are some games in stores that are well adapted to travel (see photo above). The selection generally includes various types of bingo (with no loose pieces); compact sets of chess, checkers, and cribbage packaged for traveling; assorted paper punch-out sets with patterns to complete (and no scissors needed). Most store-sold games aren't specifically meant for traveling, but by adapting some of them to special uses you can produce useful pastimes for travelers.

Adding travel features to games takes a little time. For that reason, it is suggested that parents do not wait until the eve of the vacation for game fixing and shopping. Wise use of time *before* the rush of travel preparations will guarantee happier vacationing for young and old.

ALPHABET DICE GAME

This is a variation of the "Scrabble" type dice game. In it: two sets of alphabet dice (in plastic cups with covers), two pizza pans covered with felt (to eliminate clatter of dice and glare of metal), a 3-minute egg timer with 1 and 2-minute marks on it.

Cover the pans with rubber cement and put down the felt (it will take more time than you might suspect to do a neat job), and the game is practically finished. Just enclose it in a polyethylene bag with zipper closing and it's ready to travel. Devise your own rules for this game, adjusting the degree of difficulty to ages involved. The game at left in the photo above is set up for an airplane trip. Words are restricted to those pertaining to air travel—jet, pilot, wing, and the like. Each player is allowed a certain time which is measured with the egg timer.

COOKY SHEET DRAWING BOARD

The board is an aluminum cooky sheet, spray-coated with green paint. Use at least three coats, rubbing with steel wool between coats.

Other equipment includes: a two-layer crayon box, a crayon-pencil sharpener that will hold the shavings, a pencil with a metal point cover, plastic ruler-lettering stencil, an eraser, and a sketch pad. The crayon box is glued to the board, the pencil sharpener is tied to the spiral binding of the sketch pad, pencil and eraser are tied to the cooky sheet. A large clamp holds the sketch pad. The whole thing fits into a pillowcase-size, plastic, zippered bag.

CHECKERS IN CAKE TIN

Use felt and rubber cement to cover the pan. Secure the checkers containers—plastic typewriter ribbon cases or

Ready-to-go games from stores include these always-popular favorites (clockwise from top right): stop watch, wax paper slate, bingo, punch-out set.

something similar—and the playing board in the same way. Also add score pad and pencil if you wish.

PRIZES

Playing games is even more fun if there's a prize in the offing now and then. You might collect a few whimsical and curious items that would perk up a restless young traveler at the day's end. If a prize will hold your child's attention for a time, it does double service. A Chinese puzzle (50 cents) or a wind velocity measure ($5) will be good for many miles. Other choices are picture books applicable to the area you are traveling through or books that describe historical personages or events of the countryside. Anything that moves a child's sense of the ridiculous is fun for everybody—Chinese fortune cookies or riddle books, for instance.

For a complete vacation supply of crafts items, tiny games, and books for the younger child, see page 74. Everything is kept compact in a single, plastic paper-covered shoe box.

Prizes — if they're surprises too — appeal to tired travelers. Good choices: puzzles, books, wind velocity measure, oddments with a whimsical touch.

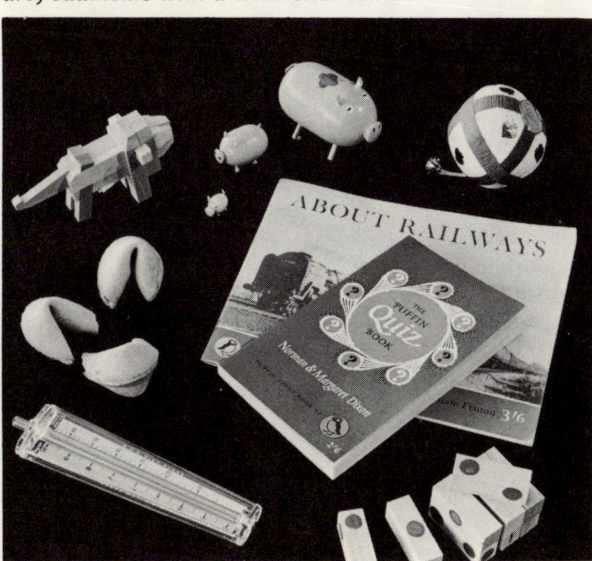

COINS AND STAMPS

Foreign coins of silver, copper, and brass jingling on her wrist will be a favorite possession of a teen-ager.

MONEY BRACELET

A handful of coins left over from a foreign trip and made into a bracelet will be a sure-fire hit with girls—especially teen-agers. Make a small hole in each coin with a metal drill. Then attach them to a link bracelet using small metal loops ("jump rings," available in hobby shops).

For a younger child's bracelet, use smaller coins than the heavy ones shown here. Coins of various metals and from several countries hold special interest. This bracelet has coins from Mexico, Central American countries, and Canada.

FOREIGN STAMPS

When you're in foreign lands, load post cards and letters to collectors at home with the small denomination stamps

Load a postcard from abroad with stamps to start a collection for a child at home. Don't overlap stamps.

that seldom get used in international mail. If you wish to splurge, use big denominations—no post office will stop a letter because of too much postage. The photograph above shows how one traveler got seven San Marino stamps on one post card. Don't risk damaging stamps by overlapping.

57

WORKSHOP PROJECTS

A ROLLING LEMONADE STAND

Warm weather brings out the homemade lemonade stands — they sprout suddenly like mushrooms, and disappear just as quickly when the lemonade has all been consumed (by customer or proprietor). For most children, a once-a-summer shot at the business world is enough, but occasionally there is the child who is a semi-steady sidewalk salesman. For those youngsters who want something permanent — and movable — here is a stand that Dad can build quite easily.

First, make a rectangular frame to fit the top of the wagon. Using 1 by 8-inch lumber, build the frame 16½ by 27 inches — or whatever size will securely overlap and rest on the wagon's sides. Next, inside the frame at each corner, nail a 1 by 2-inch by 5-foot upright for the four posts.

Now build a frame for the top, 16½ by 27 inches, using 1 by 2-inch pieces, glued and nailed. Nail frame in place around posts, 12 inches down from top of posts.

Business is brisk for this store because it can be pulled around the neighborhood on its wagon base. Gingham-covered plank set across box frame provides extra counter space. Crepe paper decorations add gay note.

Every child takes great pride in being able to say "My Dad built it for me." He likes the idea that someone as important as his father made a scooter or a bench or a clothestree *personally for him!*
- **LEMONADE STAND** on wheels.
- **SAND TABLE** that moves indoors.
- **SMALL BOAT** for a swimming pool.
- **SCOOTER** made with roller skates.
- **BASKETBALL BACKBOARD** — "pint-size."
- **CLIMBING POLE** — easy and safe.
- **BIKE PARKING:** Three ideas.
- **SECRET PANEL** for mysterious collections.
- **WORKBENCH:** Junior-size, but complete.
- **OTHER IDEAS,** including a scrap-lumber fleet and a wheel(s)barrow.

Select a large cardboard carton as near the size of the frames as possible. With a knife, cut down the carton to 6 inches in height, turn it upside-down, and cut holes where the posts will come through. This canopy and the bottom frame are easily and gaily decorated with crepe paper stretched tautly and taped. Wrap posts with crepe paper and letter the names of wares on little pennants to fly atop the posts. Tie up wagon handle with heavy twine to top of front posts; attach flags. If stand should appear top-heavy, tie a strap of canvas or heavy cloth under the wagon and up over the sides to secure it before decorating with crepe paper.

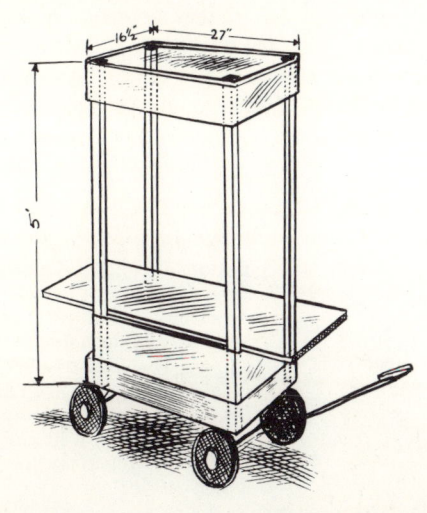

Sand box is coffee table height. It can be brought indoors, although weight of sand necessitates a two-man carry.

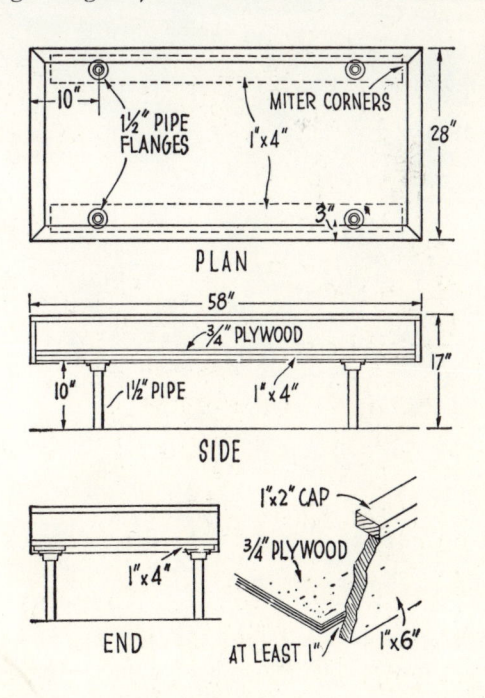

COMPACT SAND TABLE

A sand table of compact dimensions can be very useful as a child's second sand box for rainy day fun in the garage, lanai, or porch. It might also go right into the family room or the child's own room. In this case, build the sides higher and keep the sand level lower. In any instance, parents will have to accept a certain amount of sand spilling. The table should be sturdy. This one has pipe legs attached to a well-braced plywood bottom. For indoor use, drive a wooden plug into the bottom of each pipe leg to avoid floor scratching.

Young skipper happily pilots his boat in charted waters of the family swimming pool. Boat is a weekend project, costs about $15.

SWIMMING POOL BOAT

A small boat for the youngsters can be an exciting change from the inner tubes and plastic air mattresses they play with in many swimming pools. Dad can make this one in his workshop in a weekend.

Be sure you use exterior grade (or marine) plywood for the boat's shell. For the supporting pieces, use any scrap wood you have on hand that will hold screws. Glue all joints with waterproof glue and finish the boat with paint or fiber glass.

There is a cleat on the bow to make the pool boat look like the real thing. With a tow rope attached, the boat can be powered by a willing landlubber at the side of the pool.

Since the sharp prow might be a hazard to swimmers, use the boat only when the pool isn't crowded. A rubber bumper on the front will save both the prow and pool from scars. Keep the boat out of the pool when not in use and refinish it once a year to keep it from waterlogging.

The boat was designed by William King, Jr., of Honolulu.

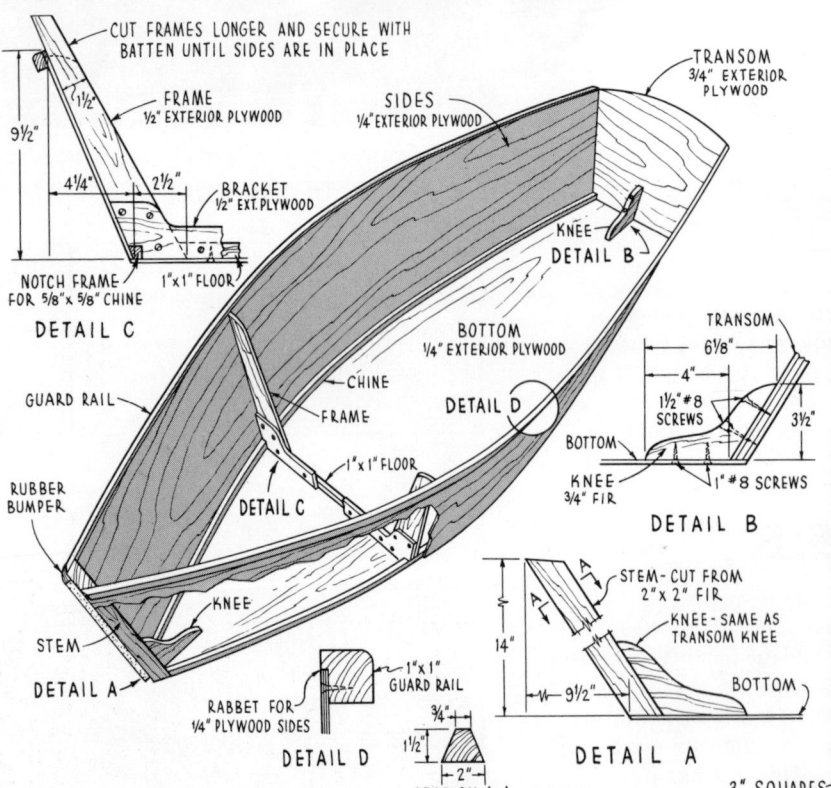

Parts and materials:
Bottom—¼-inch exterior plywood
Sides (2)—¼-inch exterior plywood
Transom—¾-inch exterior plywood
Stem—2 by 2-inch fir
Chines (2)—⅝ by ⅝-inch fir
Guard rails—1 by 1-inch fir
Frame—½-inch exterior plywood
Floor—1 by 1-inch fir
Brackets—½-inch plywood scraps
Knees—¾-inch fir

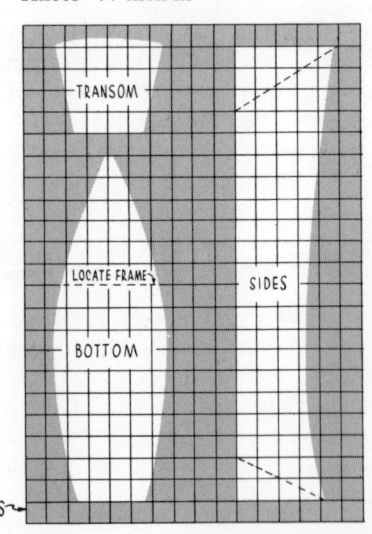

Construction details. Completed boat has overall length of 63 inches. Be sure child knows how to swim — boat is tippable.

When exterior plywood bottom, stem, and transom are cut, fit side on boat, trim excess.

THIS SCOOTER RIDES ON ROLLER SKATES

Remember the fun you once had with a soapbox scooter? Here is a modern version that will bring just as much joy to your children.

This new model is much lighter in weight, easier to handle, yet is just as bumpy and noisy — to a child, perfect! The biggest advantage is that your youngster does not need to relinquish or disassemble his roller skates to have this scooter. He simply pulls out their leather straps and clamps the skates on with his skate key. Later he can detach them in a minute and go roller skating again.

The construction requires a minimum of help from Dad — a nine-year-old can just about build the scooter himself. One ¾ by 6 by 30-inch piece of plywood (or a 1 by 6 board) provides the base, a similar piece 28 inches long constitutes the front.

First cut four notches in the base for the skate clamps. Then join the two boards together, bracing them with two ¼-inch plywood gussets, large enough to extend back past the forward notches in the base. You can jig-saw the plywood gussets to any design desired. Last, attach the two "heels" and the handlebar. Use *both* glue and nails everywhere.

This scooter gives an extra use for roller skates (they are detachable). For best steering, you have only two wheels of each skate touching the ground.

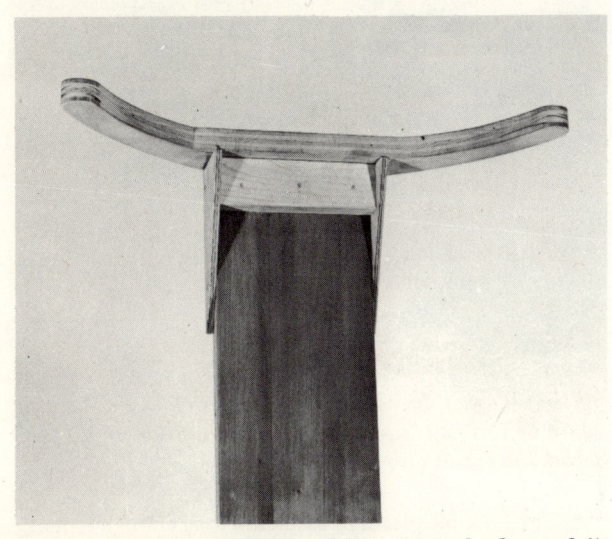

Curved handlebar is jig-sawed from ¾-inch plywood (it could be a straight piece). Be sure to brace it well.

Cut notches to receive skate clamps, at both ends of base. Wood heel fits under skate, carries all the weight.

61

The reduced height of this roll-around hoop and standard will prove welcome to a very young basketball player whose reach doesn't match his enthusiasm.

"TAILOR-MADE" FOR FIVE-YEAR-OLD BOYS

ROLL-AROUND HOOP
Five to seven-year-old basketball players will enjoy the game more if they have a backboard and hoop lowered in proportion to their height. An excellent feature of this roll-around hoop is that it may be stored out of sight in a service yard—or rolled out on a lawn or driveway for active play. Buy hoop, net, and wheels at a sporting goods store. Build of 2 by 3's and plywood.

CLIMBING POLE
What do you do for a 5-year-old who likes to climb? One answer is this safe climbing pole placed in a play yard. The pole is 4 by 4-inch redwood, 11 feet long, sunk 2 feet into the ground. For the rungs, use ¾-inch dowels 8½

If a play yard (or grandparents' back yard) doesn't have a suitable tree for climbing, build a climbing pole.

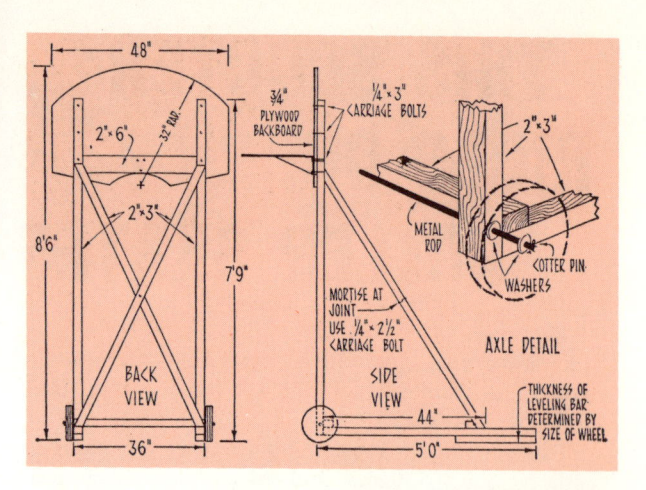

inches long, set 12 inches apart on alternate sides of the pole. Drill the holes 2 inches deep, at a slight angle so that small feet tend to slide toward the pole. Dowels are glued in place.

The boy in the photo below helped stain his pole a dark gray-green that blends with the garden background. The pole was finished with spar varnish to prevent splinters.

NOISY STILTS
Turn two empty 46-ounce juice cans upside-down and make 2 holes in opposite sides of each can just below the

These tin-can stilts can give a younger child the exciting sense of walking "up high." They are easier to use than wood stilts, and also much safer.

lid. Cut 2 double pieces of sash cord long enough to make handles. Use a piece of wire to thread cord through holes; then knot the ends.

A bike parking rack will help avoid clutter on your lawn or driveway. Top, bottom crosspieces give 5-inch hold on front wheel.

BIKE RACK IDEAS

FAMILY BIKE PARKING
If there is a bicycle or two already in your family and another birthday to come, a rack like this may be in order. Such a parking point is a real help in avoiding the cluttered look that bikes can

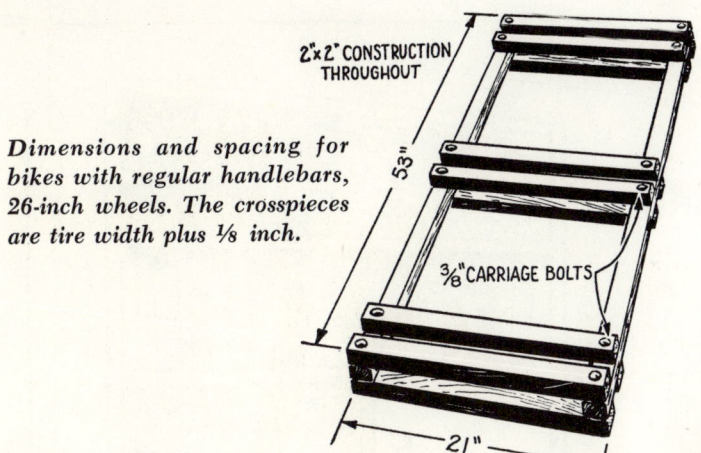

Dimensions and spacing for bikes with regular handlebars, 26-inch wheels. The crosspieces are tire width plus 1/8 inch.

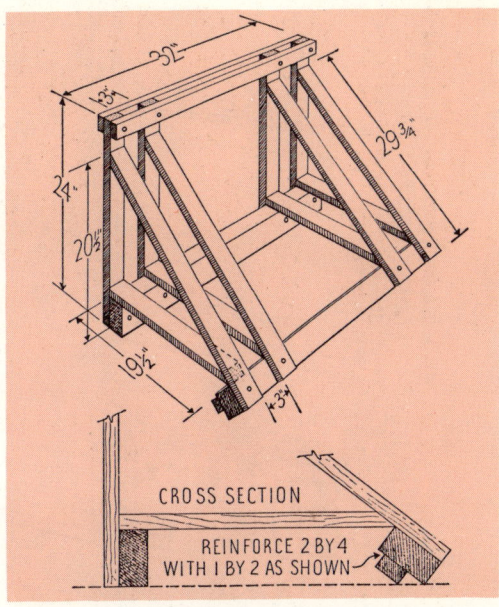

give a car port or yard. The rack shown here is one you can easily make at a cost of about $4. The design may be enlarged to make a rack for more bikes. Glue crosspieces in place on side pieces for stability. They should be placed a tire width plus 1/8-inch apart. Then bolt the crosspieces through side pieces as shown. Let bolts protrude if rack will be on the ground; recess them if the rack will be on a paved area. This will prevent scarring.

FREE-STANDING RACK
This rack is portable. Built from 1 by 2-inch lumber, except for the two 2 by 4-inch base pieces, this rack was designed as a building project for a den of Cub Scouts. All cuts are right angles except for those on the horizontal and angular bracing. Make these simple angle cuts by holding members in position and then marking off cuts with a pencil. Twelve 1/4-inch carriage bolts and washers, in positions shown in drawing, make the sturdiest structure. Nail other members with four-penny nails. Here is the lumber you'll need:

Number	Length	Dimension
2	32 inches	2 by 4's
3	32 inches	1 by 2's
4	19½ inches	1 by 2's
4	24 inches	1 by 2's
4	29¾ inches	1 by 2's

Shelter for three bikes was achieved by cutting slots in fence that forms part of a car port wall. Slat on paving holds wheels.

FOR TRINKETS AND TREASURES ...A SECRET PANEL

Secret panels hold a special fascination for children. The hidden compartment on the left, although it is only 3½ inches deep, can hold a wide variety of small objects—toys, sketches, photographs, and hobby collections, to name just a few.

The panel is simply a small section of removable wall that is held in at the bottom by the baseboard and at the top by a hinged facing board that swings out and up so the panel can be removed or reinserted. In order that the panel may be locked, cut a vertical slot in the facing board and drive a large staple through it to slip the lock through. Curtains hide the lock.

When cutting into the wall, be certain to leave part of the stud exposed on each side so the panel will have something to lean against. As a safety precaution, make certain there is no electrical wiring inside the wall where you plan to work.

Wallpaper scraps or samples can be used to decorate the interior, and the decor can be changed at will.

...A LOCK-UP SHELF FOR TRUCKS AND TRAINS

A bookcase can be remodeled to make an excellent "garage" for toy cars or a "hangar" for airplanes.
Remove the next-to-bottom shelf and the one above it. Cut a groove in the bottom of the upper shelf and the top of the lower one—each about ½ inch in from the front—wide enough to accommodate a sliding door of thin plywood. Make the door half the width of the bookcase; attach a simple knob handle. Replace the shelves, this time with door fitted into grooves. (Space shelves so the door slides easily yet will not pull loose.) Using nails or epoxy glue, insert a divider in the center of the shelf; when cars and planes are not in use, they may be placed all on one side of the shelf and hidden from view by the sliding door.

As an added touch, a boy will enjoy racing his cars down a simple plywood ramp (of optional length) which can be stored out of sight behind the bookcase.

Here is a father-to-son gift, for birthday or Christmas, that is certain to be a smashing success: His own workbench, plus a cabinet stocked with basic tools.

GIFT FOR A BOY: HIS OWN WORKBENCH

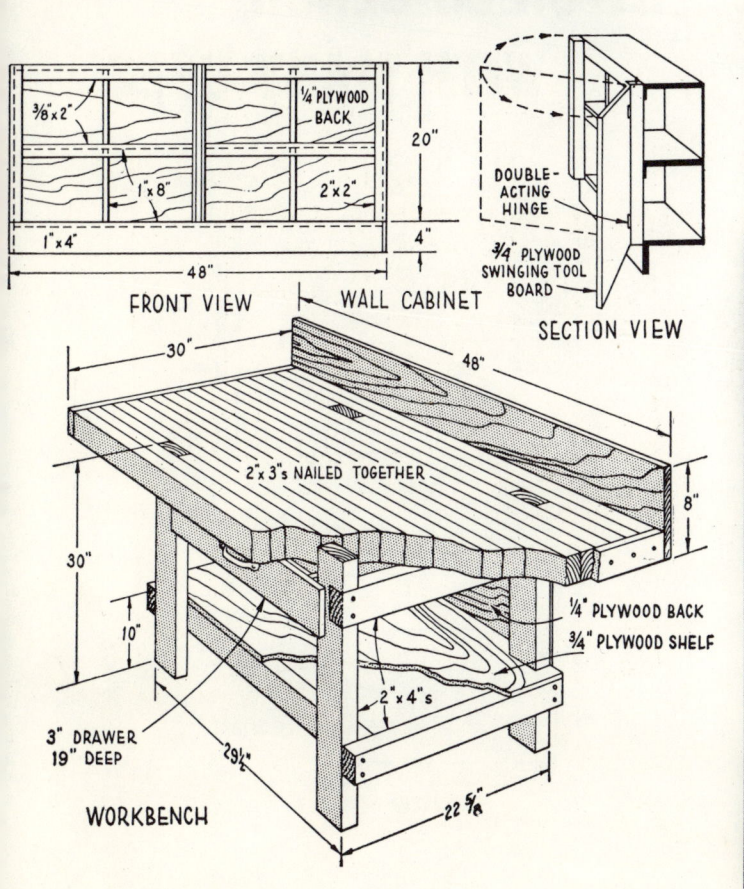

For your young son there is no better way of becoming interested in crafts than to have his own workbench. This one is as sturdy as his Dad's—only smaller. An ideal workbench, it gives the child his own work space, with room to store his tools and half-finished projects. His building and craft work won't be scattered around the garage or house, and the space of his own will be an incentive to finish each job.

This workbench was made from 2 by 4's and 2 by 3's, with the lower storage shelf and back of plywood. Construction is simple, requiring only the common tools found in most home workshops. The laminated top is tough enough to take almost any treatment your young son can dish out. He'll also find it a good working surface for small craft jobs like building model airplanes.

The wall cabinet above needs no door. Instead, it has a pivoting center leaf for hanging hand tools so they are always in plain sight. Screw-in cup hooks and tool or broom clamps will hold almost any size tool. To make the set-up complete, stock the cabinet with some of the basic hand tools he'll need.

Secure cabinet to the wall with ten-penny nails driven through plywood back and into the wall studs. Shelves hold jars of tacks and nails, glue, paint, tools.

THIS FLEET SAILS THE PLAYROOM FLOOR

This floor fleet includes eight types of craft. Materials needed are inexpensive: 1 by 3, 1 by 4, and 2 by 4 pieces of scrap lumber; plywood; cardboard; dowels of different sizes; bits of a clothes-closet pole. Paint the fleet with airplane paint or general-purpose paint in bright colors.

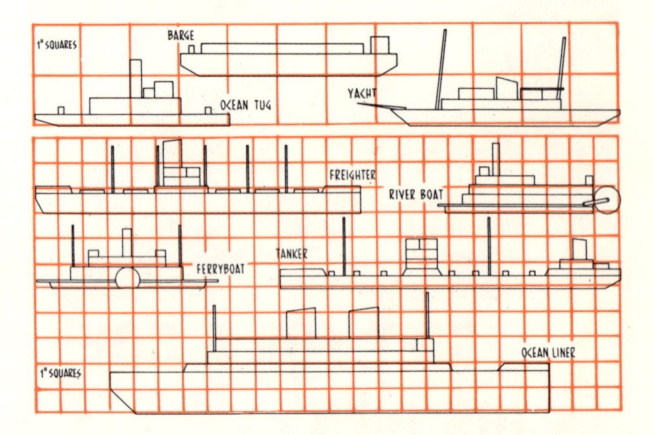

River boats and ships are in accurate scale — 3 inches to 100 feet. Designs kept simple for easy construction.

TOT-SIZED BENCH WITH MANY USES

Four cord-and-wood benches like this were originally made for children to use around the fireplace while popping corn. Since then they have been put to numerous other uses — as doll beds, as train cars linked together and pushed, as seats around a play table. "Upholstery" is seiner's twine, but any good cord would be satisfactory. The finish is white filler rubbed in, with a coat of lacquer on top.

Small cord-and-wood bench may be stored easily under larger furniture and has a variety of child-tested uses.

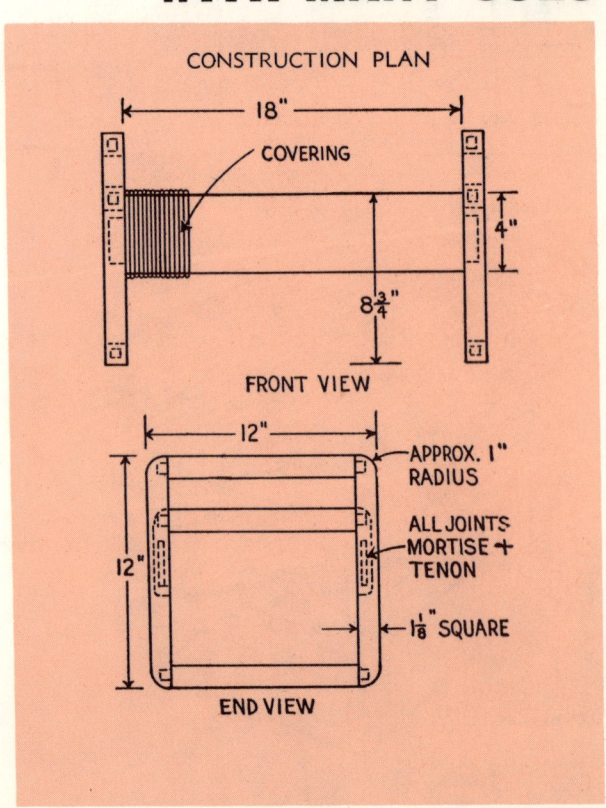

66

THREE WHIMSICAL CLOTHESTREES

BIRD HOUSE TREE

It is more fun to hang a jacket on a clothestree than it is to put it in the closet. For this whimsical bird house you will need 4 feet of closet pole and 5½ feet of ¾-inch wood doweling, plus a flat piece of ¾-inch plywood from which you cut the shoe shelf.

Spiral as many holes around the pole as you want hangers. Shortest hanger is 3 inches; each higher one is ½ inch longer. With a ¾-inch bit, drill the hanger holes and shelf leg holes. Rasp and sandpaper one end of each hanger. You will need an expansion bit to drill a hole in the plywood shelf to accept the closet pole. Cut pole and legs to a desired length. Assemble the tree with strong glue. Varnish or paint.

Giraffe is 45 inches tall, hoof to ear tip; it will not tip when hung with clothes.

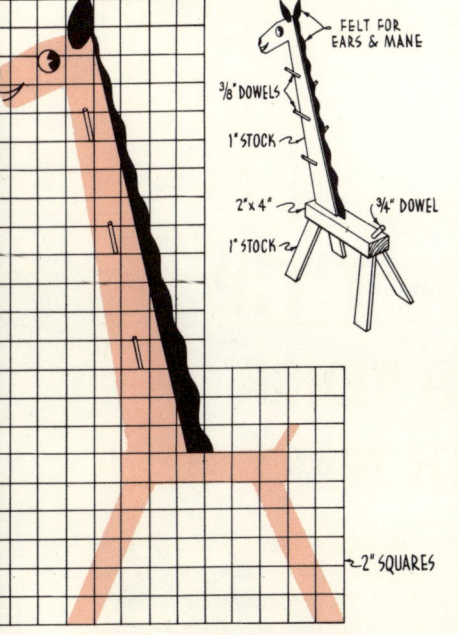

GIRAFFE TREE

To make the giraffe clothestree, you will need 12 inches of 2 by 4-inch scrap lumber for the body; 1-inch stock for the neck, head, legs; ⅜-inch dowels for the pegs and tail; a 2 by 36-inch piece of felt for the mane and ears; glue; and paint in several colors.

Since the giraffe has no curved pieces you don't have any tedious saw work. With the standard blade of a circular saw, make a cut up the back of the neck piece. Use a screwdriver to push the felt mane into this slit. Put the dado blade on the saw and make cuts for the legs in the base piece. Drill holes for the dowels with a brace and bit or electric drill. After you glue in the dowels and legs, paint the clothestree to suit your idea of what a giraffe should look like.

PACK HORSE

Here is a clotheshorse which handles shoes as well as stray coats and shirts. The ears and tail of the completed horse are made from hangers screwed into the head and the body. Over the body, hang a gingham saddle bag for shoes and slippers. Build the horse with the following material: 4 by 4-inch block for the body; 2 by 4-inch pieces of scrap lumber for feet and head; any desired lengths of closet pole for legs; 1-inch dowel for neck; and smaller dowel for braces. Feet may be cut any shape you wish. Shape head and sandpaper edges. With an expansion bit, bore holes for legs, neck, and braces. Firmly glue all joints. Paint and decorate.

In place of bird house perched on clothestree you might choose a stuffed koala.

Clotheshorse sports shoe bags for saddle. The ears and tail are coat hooks.

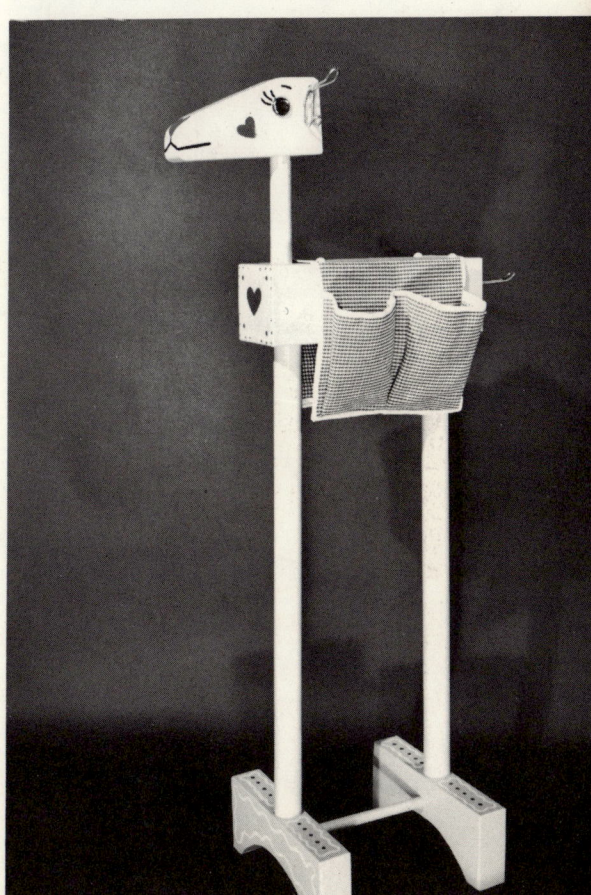

A young outdoor workman can use this easy-to-build two-wheeled barrow to help Daddy haul leaves or grass.

Two wheels give this boy's wheelbarrow far more stability than the conventional one-wheeler has. It is scaled down to a size suitable for young garden helpers, and it holds enough leaves or grass to make a 4 or 5-year-old feel important. He could even give his baby sister a safe whirl around the yard.

This wheelbarrow was built from plywood, a pair of wagon wheels, and an axle (see diagram below). (Most sporting goods stores sell wagon wheels, or you might be able to salvage a pair from a worn-out wagon or tricycle.) It is easily built with ordinary hand tools. Perhaps the child could help to paint it in the colors of his choice.

FOR A BOY:
A WHEELBARROW THAT WON'T TIP

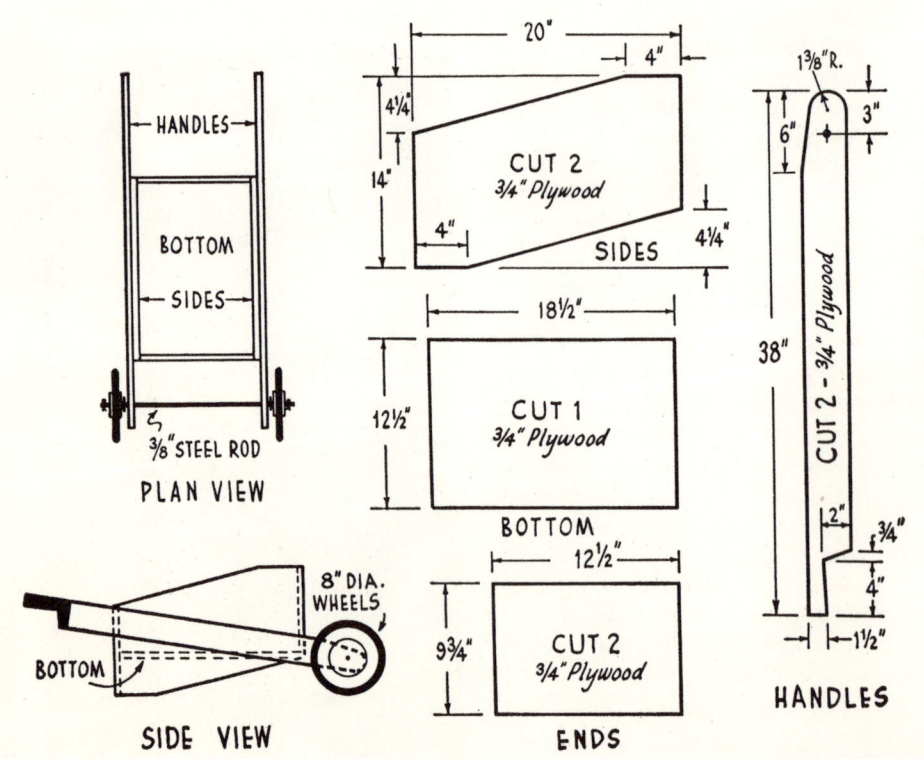

After building one of these sturdy little barrows for his son, Dad might well be sufficiently impressed to wish he had one similar to it for himself. It's easy — just increase dimensions to size desired and use larger wheels. Front could be slanted for easier dumping. Barrow is not meant to carry heavy loads.

Any girl who likes old-fashioned doll furniture would be delighted to possess this ante-bellum four-poster. The careful details and lovely design of the bed could well make it one of your child's favorites — possibly leading to a hobby of antique-design miniatures.

Made of pine, it is stained and varnished. A small pillow of striped mattress ticking, stuffed 2 inches thick with cotton batting, serves as the mattress. Both bedspread and canopy in the photo are taffeta. A cotton print in small floral design or tiny checks would also be appropriate.

The plan below gives construction details. If you do not have a lathe, you might do the shaping work in a public school or other workshop available for public use. The pieces are small, so you can easily transport them home.

Here's a surprise for a young girl: a large doll bed.

FOR A GIRL:
A FOUR-POSTER DOLL BED

This piece of doll furniture is unusual in its very careful detail. Join pieces of the bed with both dowels and glue. Use a band saw to cut two curved pieces of canopy.

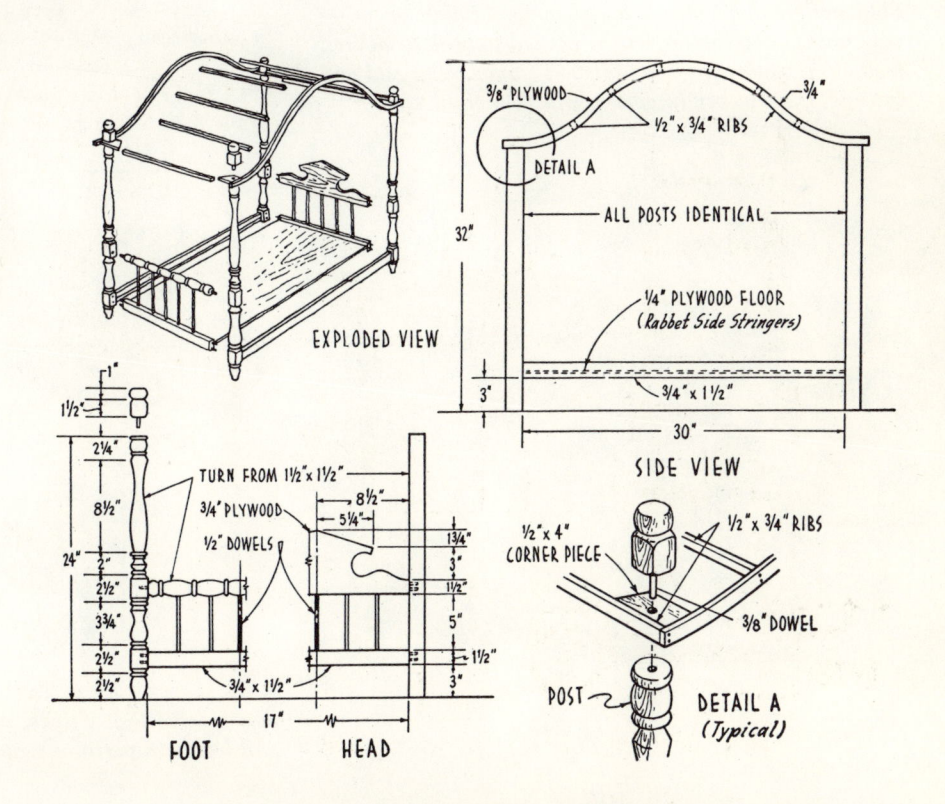

69

ART CRAFTS

A COLORFUL PAPER JUNGLE

FOR ROOM OR PARTY

These animal "trophies" are fun to create, temporary, and inexpensive. Make them of construction paper for a nursery, for an older child's room — or for a party. You'll need scissors, paste, 12 by 18-inch construction paper, a metal-edged ruler, and a blunt craft knife or single-edged razor blade.

In the patterns shown the dash lines show where to score paper; solid lines, where to cut; dotted lines, where to paste. Use the craft knife to score paper, bearing down only enough to break the top fibers so it will fold easily. (See page 12 for paper sculpture techniques.)

Bold patterns on bulletin board make a jungle scene — cut-outs of construction paper, pinned to burlap-covered insulating wallboard in a redwood frame. Wise owl and intrepid tiger in bright colors appeal to children.

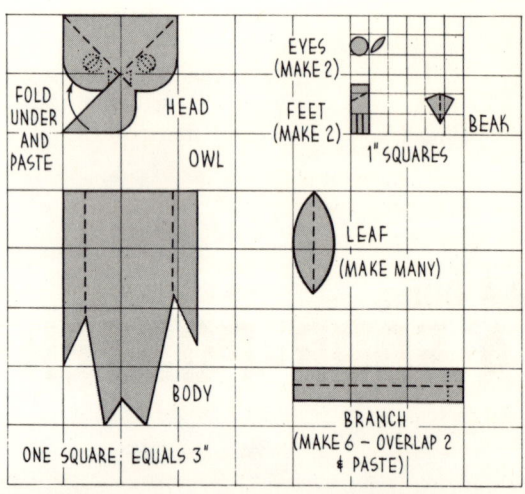

Curl owl's feet on back of ruler; hook them over tree branch. Fold wings outward. Simple fold for leaves.

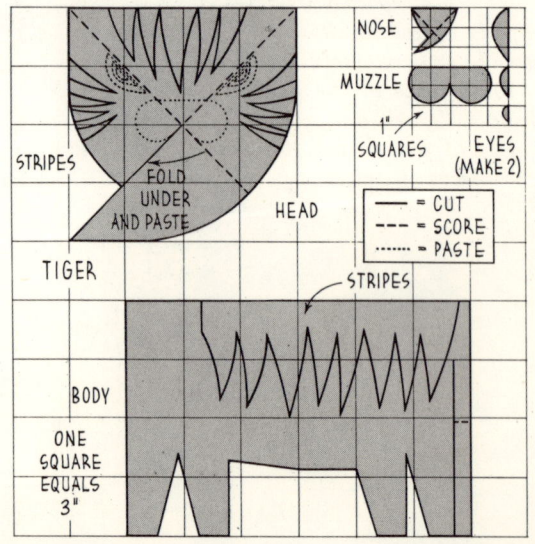

Cut contrasting stripes, paste to tiger's head and body. All heads in patterns may be enlarged for masks.

There is no surer way to develop a child's interest in crafts than to tackle a craft project yourself, with the child becoming the proud owner of the finished product. If the youngster is allowed to help out with a simple task or two, so much the better. Here is a varied assortment of handcraft projects, none of which take special skills.

- **PAPER CUT-OUTS**: Tigers, owls, purple elephants, pink giraffes...
- **CRAFT KIT** for a young craftsman.
- **SPRAY-STENCILS**: Chickens on burlap.
- **HANDBAGS**: Just decorate a basket...
- **COOKY CROCK**: You paint it to match your gingerbread cookies.
- **PARAFFIN CANDLES**. Other ideas, too...

Make heads and bodies of animals from flat sheets of paper, scoring and folding to simulate wrinkles. From contrasting colors cut out eyes, stripes, spots, and decorations; paste in place. Accordion-pleat the grasses and cut the tops to represent spears. Be as frivolous as you wish—have a purple elephant with blue head, ears, and toes; try a pink giraffe with magenta spots.

In attaching the paper cut-outs to surfaces such as a bulletin board, place straight pins in at an angle. They are less apt to be pulled out. (It's a good idea to keep a *pinned* trophy high above the reach of toddlers.) To attach cut-outs to walls, use double-faced tape, or a small strip of masking tape or cellophane tape rolled into a ring.

All designs are by William J. Shelley.

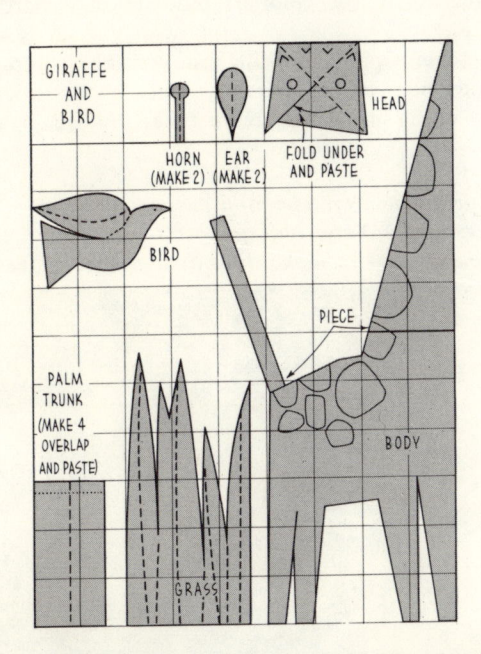

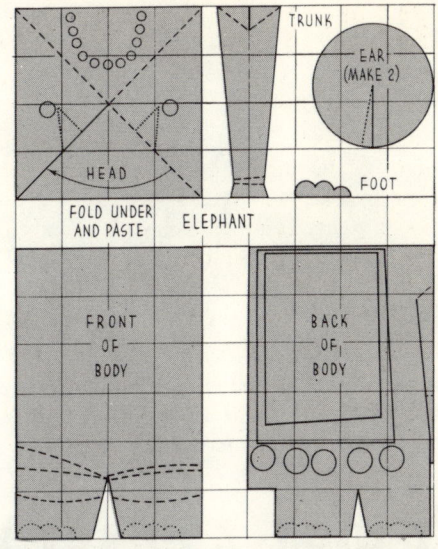

Curl elephant's trunk over ruler or back of scissors. Score knees for wrinkles; add ears, toes, decorations.

Jungle on a wall — a purple elephant eyes a tall giraffe while bluebirds fly overhead. Tree, grasses are "tropical."

Piece giraffe together as shown. Fold horns and ears lengthwise; insert them in slits cut in elongated head.

Generous supply of butcher paper encourages artist to paint with freedom. Mount 24-inch-wide roll in store-counter cutter. Roll, 1,250 feet, costs about $8.

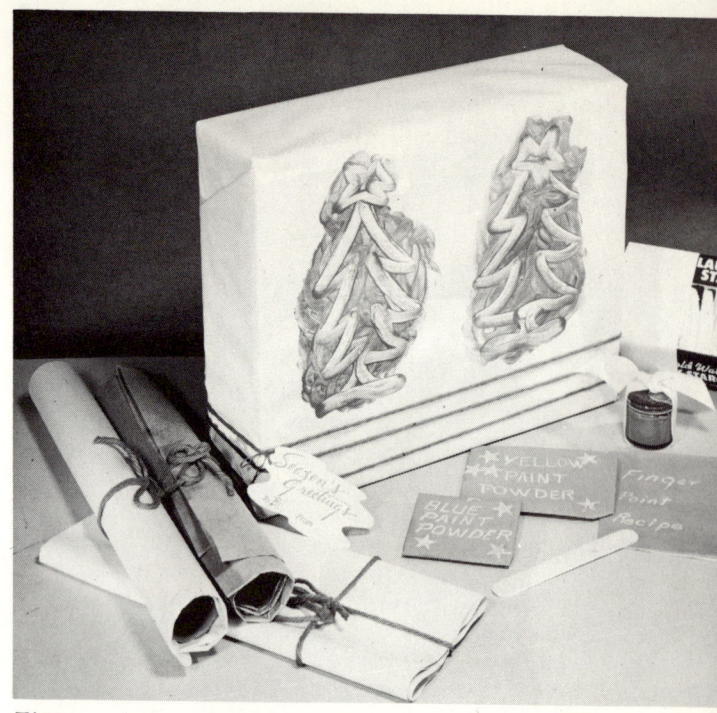

Finger painting set: Paper, oil cloth to protect table, paint powders, starch and recipe (see below).

GIFT IDEA: A CRAFT KIT

A gift which a child hasn't thought to ask for is often one which will appeal the most. Young artists will delight in an unknown, undiscovered present made up of paints, paper, or craft supplies which you have organized in one gift.

Three packages of this type are shown here. The huge roll of butcher paper encourages the youngster to turn out literally hundreds of drawings. The box full of yarn, burlap scraps, poster paint, and brushes is for three-dimensional pictures.

The finger painting set is wrapped in decorated oil cloth and contains rolls of butcher paper, more oil cloth to protect the table, packets of paint powders, starch for mixing, and the finger paint recipe, as follows:

> 1¼ cups laundry starch
> Cold water
> 3 cups of boiling water
> ½ cup soap flakes
> 1 teaspoon glycerine or alum

Mix starch with enough cold water to make a smooth paste. Add mixture to boiling water, cool for ½ minute, then stir in soap flakes while mixture is still hot. Beat until creamy and thick. Add glycerine or alum and pour into jars. The children add dry powdered colors from salt shakers to the colorless paste as they start their pictures.

Butcher paper takes paint best. Wet sheets thoroughly on both sides before painting. Place about two tablespoons of the starch mixture on a sheet for each painting.

Gift for a young craftsman: a package wrapped in part of its contents. Yarn, burlap, poster paint, brushes, colored paper used to make three-dimensional pictures.

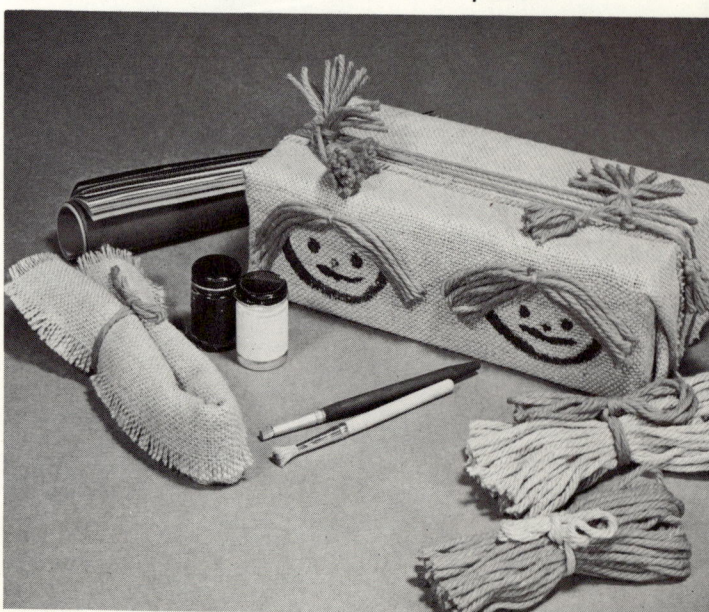

72

Busy hens on burlap panel stenciled with paper patterns sprayed with pressurized paint. The "feathers" are small bits of hardware.

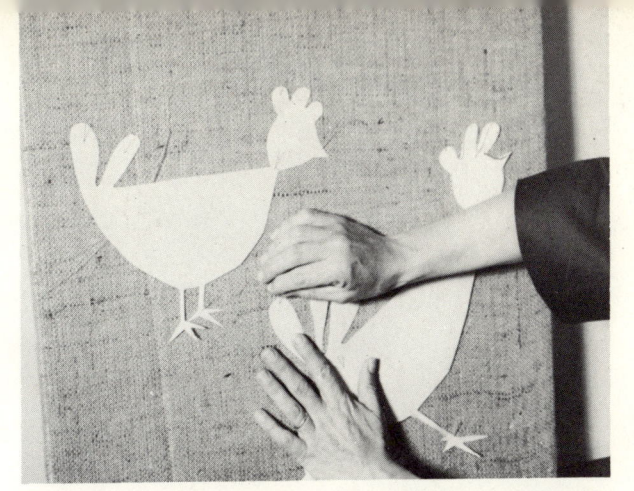

1. Tightly tack burlap over fiberboard. Affix chicken wire. Fasten paper patterns to the panel with enough pins so the edges are close against the burlap.

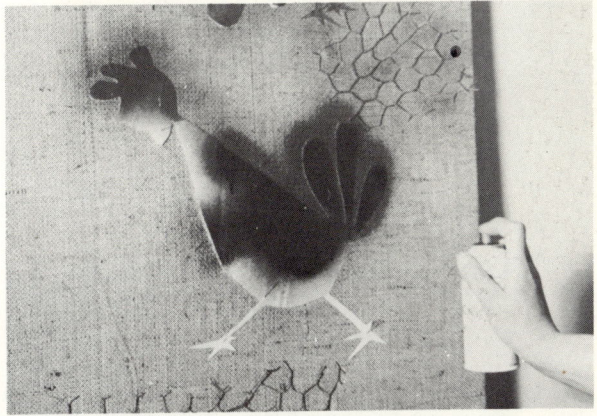

2. Hold pressurized can of paint a foot from the panel. Spray a fairly heavy layer around pattern edges; then feather out for several inches.

3. Remove patterns and chicken wire when paint dries. Decorate hens with metal and bone rings fastened to the board with staples and tacks.

WHIMSY ON A WALL

Busy hens parading on a burlap panel add a note of whimsy to the wall of a child's room. Cover a 2 by 5-foot panel of soft fiberboard with natural colored burlap. The patterns are spray-stenciled in black and decorated with odds and ends from a hardware store—metal, bone, and rubber rings and washers; upholstery tacks and thumb tacks.

You will need the following materials: fiberboard; enough burlap to cover, plus a 1½-inch overlap; pressurized can of paint; pins; washers and tacks; paper patterns. Pieces of chicken wire, tacked between the patterns, add texture. Spray patterns and wire, then remove. Use strips of molding for the frame.

FOR YOUNG TRAVELERS... A SHOE BOX FULL OF SURPRISES

More than a dozen wonderful playthings fill this shoebox, and each can mean a long period of happy play for a child on a rainy day or during a long trip. Cover the box with sticky-back plastic paper, and identify it by placing the owner's name on the lid.

In this box (for an 8-year-old boy) is included a large box of crayons; magnifying glass; pieces of colored paper; compass; scratch pad; sticky tape; blunt scissors; small games; color book; road maps; plastic tube of glue; wood clothespins and an envelope of braid, buttons, and feathers for making Indians. A pack of playing cards, a sack of balloons, and a balsa airplane can ease the confinement of a hotel or motel room. A box filled with suitable toys can also be an excellent gift for an invalid.

BEE MOBILE...

A mobile is truly a baby's first "toy." Any bright object moving gently over a crib will fascinate a tiny child and he will follow its movements with his eyes. And the interest continues as the child grows — mobiles are really "look-at" toys for all ages.

This bee of colored tissue paper and bamboo hangs overhead, suspended by string. Use 45-inch lengths of matchstick bamboo for the framework (or light wire can be easily bent into the same shape). First, soak the bamboo until it is easily flexed, bend it into shapes shown in the diagram, and wire in place. Buy bright tissue paper for a colorful bee — most variety stores have pastel shades and art shops sell brilliant, deep shades. Trace the shapes of the various bamboo forms on the tissue, leaving enough margin to firmly glue to the bamboo. After all forms have been covered with tissue, attach pieces together with wire, and suspend.

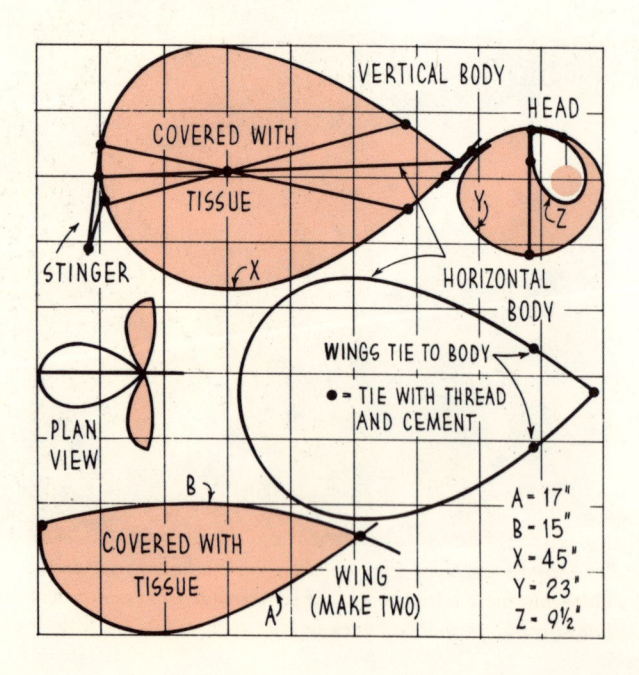

Tissue-and-bamboo bee swings gently in the air. Cover bamboo frame with colored tissue, suspend with string.

A = 17"
B = 15"
X = 45"
Y = 23"
Z = 9½"

Large lauhala matting catch-all makes handsome beach bag. Decorate with starfish, pieces of white coral, and plastic fish found in variety stores. Yellow felt handles.

Plastic grapes in cool purple are sewed to a cylindrical basket of soft, natural colored straw. Arrangements of plastic vegetables, gilded nuts are also attractive.

DECORATE A BASKET...IT'S A HANDBAG!

Gay handbag to go with young lady's summer frock is made of hinged-top basket decorated with shells and artificial flowers, finished with lacquer. Lay out the design on paper; glue, wire each piece in place on basket.

A young sophisticate would enjoy this parasol-shaped basket with bright roses of wood fiber.

Stiffen string wicks by dipping in hot paraffin melted over low heat; wax crayons may be added for color.

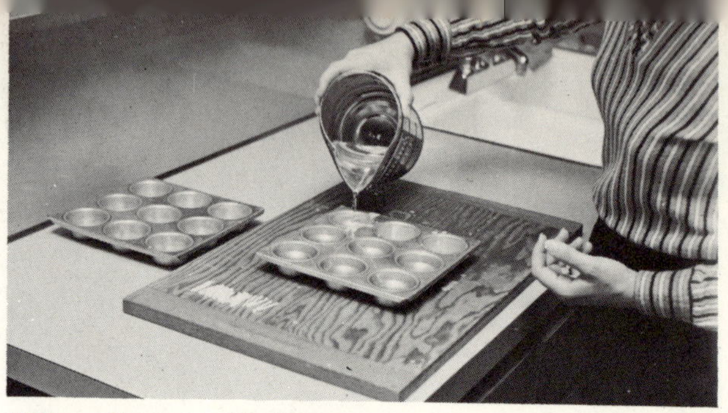

Fill muffin tins with slightly cooled liquid paraffin. Bend a coffee can rim to form a lip from which to pour.

PARAFFIN CANDLES

Making simple paraffin candles is a good project for a den of Cub Scouts or a Brownie Troop. Two pounds of paraffin makes 18 candles, muffin-size.

Push stiffened wicks into centers while the paraffin is still warm but is beginning to lose its transparency.

When candles are cool, ease them out with a table knife. You may add sequins, beads, or glitter for fancy effects.

BASKET CRADLE FOR A DOLL

A plain basket becomes a queenly bed for a doll when a canopy, mattress, and colorful pillow are added. This bed started as an 18-inch basket, but smaller baskets could also be used. Here's how to make it:

With a few embellishments, basket can be a doll bed.

Saw bases for head and foot from 1-inch boards and screw to pieces of wood fitting into the inside of the basket bottom. Holder for the canopy is made from a cut-off basket handle. Soak the handle in water for an hour and bend it into shape.

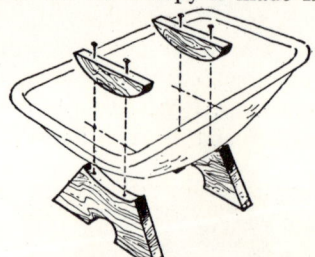

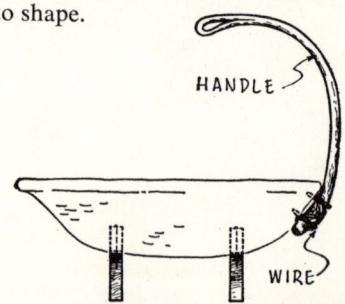

Two loops of wire, wound with raffia, hold the handle to the head of the bed.

Decorate cooky jar with plastic paint especially made for application on ceramic surfaces (buy at art supply stores in a variety of colors). Mix it like oil paint with palette knife. Brush on your own designs.

PAINT THE CROCK TO MATCH THE COOKIES

If you can make gingerbread cookies like those below, you can also make a matching cooky crock to put them in.— a special container for your children's after-school treats.

Coarse stoneware crocks, ordinarily used for watering chickens or putting up pickles or sauerkraut, make good inexpensive containers. Decorate the glazed surface with the type of plastic paint made to be cured in a kitchen oven. Buy paint at art supply or stationery stores.

Trace around cooky cutter on plain paper. Cut out the pattern and outline it on the crock with pencil. Fill in with paint, which comes in many bright colors. Follow directions on label for oven-curing. Paints are semi-permanent. These containers can stand oven heat, but placing them in the refrigerator causes the paint to peel.

Designs are cut out of heavy paper, taped around crock, and outlined. Trace cooky cutters if you wish.

Each gingerbread boy or girl design on the outside of the crock has a cooky "twin" on the inside.

SEWING

Children of all ages are sure to like this warm scarf cap. Easy to make and fun to wear, it keeps neck and ears cozy.

SURPRISE YOUR DAUGHTER WITH A SCARF CAP

This cap is ideal for a quick and easy-to-make ear warmer. It requires little or no sewing and takes only a square yard of fabric. For small children, a large bandanna will do nicely. Larger scarf-caps may be made of light weight wool, denim, or bright red flannel for a real "Little Red Riding Hood."

Finish the edges of the square with pinking shears, or make narrow hems if the fabric ravels a great deal. Make the folds shown on the opposite page, and it is ready to tie on. The final fold could be hand-tacked in several places to keep it secure when removed. A little bell or tassel attached to the peak adds a merry touch.

It is also a good idea to keep on hand a square of clear plastic to quickly fold up for an emergency rain hood. Handkerchiefs folded in this way also make very acceptable hoods for dolls of any size.

Sewing for children doesn't need to stop just with the practical. Here are ideas — all touched with whimsy, all with some little detail that will fascinate a child.
- SCARF-CAP for your "Red Riding Hood."
- SLIPPERS for all sizes of feet.
- TOY APPLIQUÉS for coveralls or skirt.
- GINGERBREAD "TRIPLETS"—coveralls and two stuffed dolls.
- SMOCK with a "sleepy bunny" pocket.
- SWEATER DECORATIONS for a girl.
- MONKEYS made of stockings.
- OTHER IDEAS: Yarn animals, pillow toys.

1. Fold the material in half. Then fold top layer in half; make edges even. Bell is in center of the square.

2. Turn down about 2½ inches of folded edge of fabric to make the face-framing cuff. Then iron in creases.

3. Turn folded fabric over, preserving creases. Pick up corners facing you and make diagonal folds in material.

4. Roll folded material from bottom of the triangle up as far as needed for snug fit. This is back of cap.

COZY SLIPPERS...

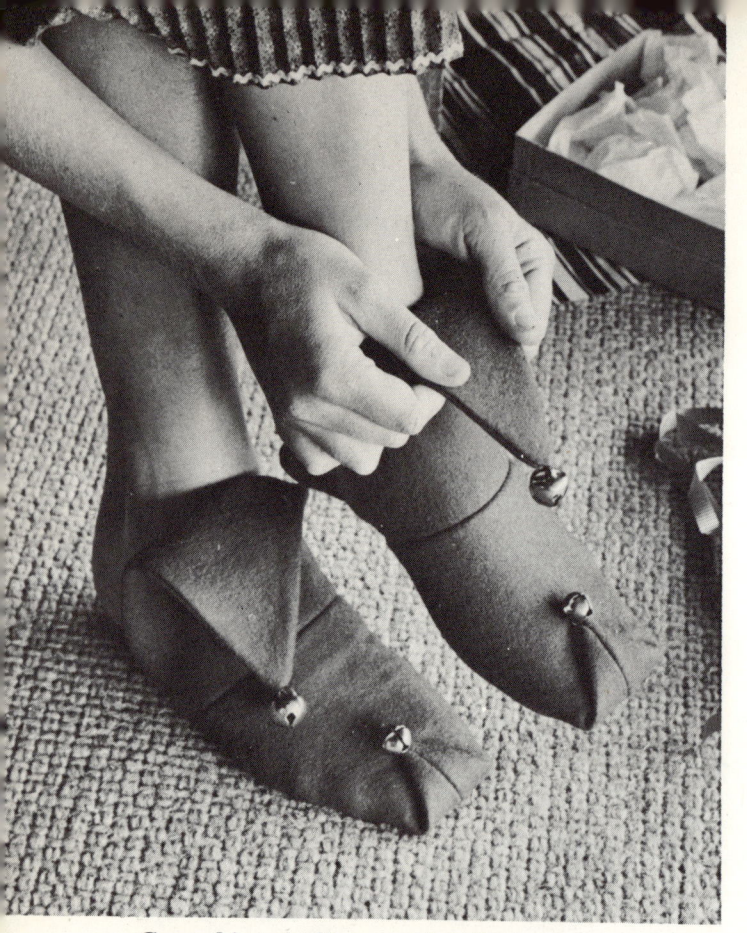

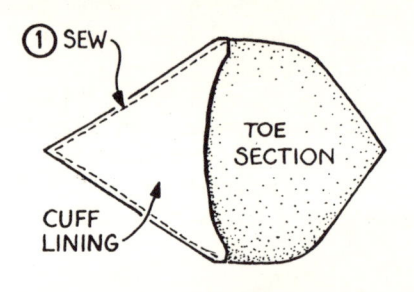

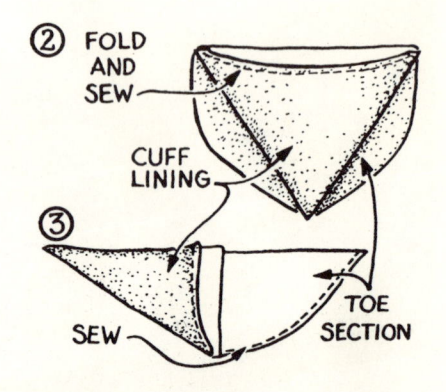

Gay red jester's slippers with bells on cuffs and toes may be made of felt or suede to fit a child's feet.

These soft jester's slippers with their jingling bells would be welcomed by a girl or a *young* boy. You can vary the pattern to match any foot.

The slippers in the above photograph were made in about 45 minutes. For a similar pair, you'll need ⅔ yard of 30 inch-wide felt or an equal amount of suede leather (slightly less for very small feet), a pair of foam rubber inner soles, and 4 small jingle bells. You can use a sewing machine for most of the sewing.

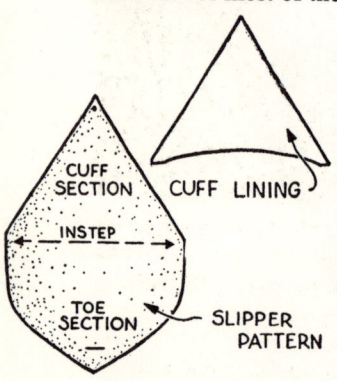

Cut out a paper pattern, following the shape in the sketch at left. If slippers are to fit snugly, you'll need two measurements of the future wearer's foot: 1) the distance around the foot, measured from one side of the instep to the other and across the sole, 2) the distance from the tip of the big toe along the bottom of the foot to the middle of instep.

The pattern should be as wide as the measurement around the instep *plus* a ⅜-inch seam on each side. Make the toe section as long as the distance from the tip of the toe to the instep plus 1½ inches and the cuff section about an inch longer than the toe section. The cuff lining should be the same size as the cuff section of the whole slipper. Use the same pattern for both right and left slippers.

Cut the pieces for both slippers. Place the cuff lining over the cuff section of the main part of the slipper, right sides together. Stitch the edges. Then turn the piece right side out and fold it in half at the instep (step 2 in the sketch above). Sew the three thicknesses of material together. Trim the seam and turn toe section right side out. Fold the cuff section over the toe section.

For soles, cut 2 pieces ⅜ inch larger all around than each inner sole. Sew sole sections together, wrong sides out, leaving a small opening for inserting inner sole. Turn right side out through opening, slip the inner sole inside, and hand stitch to close. Place toe of sole piece inside the toe section of slipper; tack the two pieces together along sides. Sew bells on tips of each cuff and each slipper toe. Fold the toe back over the rest of slipper and tack it. You may want to sew a small piece of elastic around the heel if you plan to give the slippers to a very young child.

...COOL SLIPPERS

Kona slippers are fun to make and fun to wear. The materials don't cost much and you can match prints to your daughter's pajamas or playsuit.

You'll need two patterns. As a guide, use the sole pattern below or trace a slipper outline. Then trace this pattern *twice* on a lauhala grass matting place mat. To keep edges from shredding, machine sew 1/8 inch inside the tracing line before cutting out the soles. Using the same pattern, cut 2 cardboard soles, 4 sole-shaped pieces of flannel or toweling, and 2 pieces of canvas or denim 3/4 inch larger all around than the pattern.

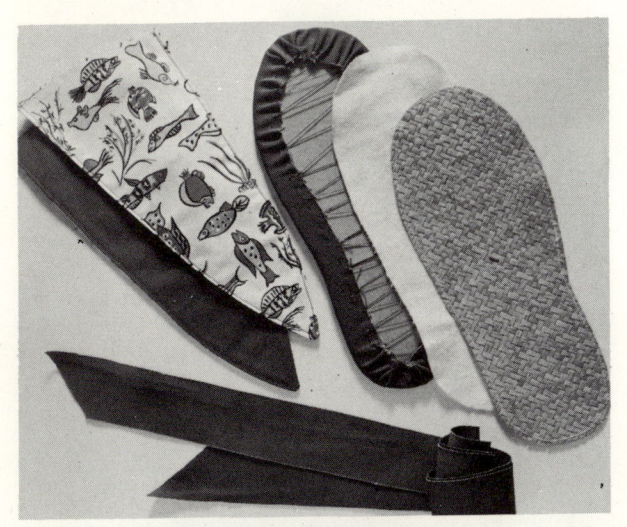

Make a toe tie pattern (see sketch); use it to cut 8 ties — 4 in solid color, 4 in print. Cut solid color bias strips 1½ inches wide and each long enough to go around a sole.

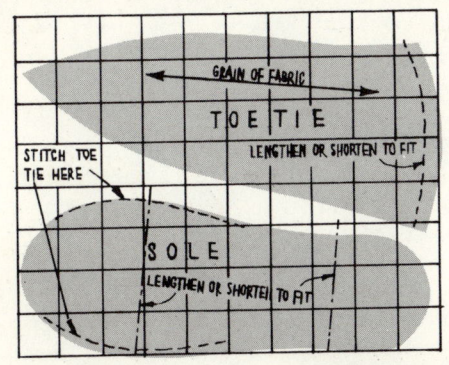

Slipper pieces (left to right): faced toe ties, bottom sole, padding, lauhala sole, bias binding.

Make sole and tie patterns on a grid of 1-inch squares.

In one morning you can make these gay Hawaiian slippers to match your daughter's printed pajamas or robe.

Assemble bottom soles first: Run a gathering thread around each piece of canvas. Then place a flannel sole in the center and top with a cardboard sole. Pull gathering thread so the heavy fabric encloses these two soles. Tie thread. Whip opposite edges of fabric together so it is tightly drawn around the cardboard.

Face the ties, right sides together. Turn right side out and stitch again close to edge. Pin ties, print side up, into place on each side of a lauhala sole. Lay binding on top of lauhala with edges together; sew binding to sole ½ inch in from edge (catch ties in binding, too). Turn sole over; place one flannel sole against bottom. Pull binding around

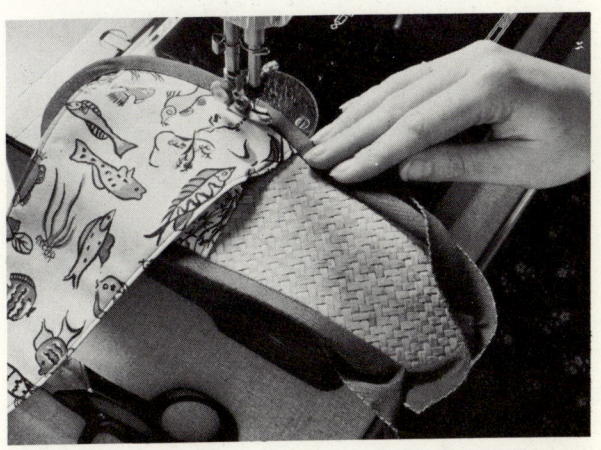

Top-stitch inside edge of binding when you sew around sole the second time; at the same time, you catch the raw edge of the binding on the underside of the sole.

these soles and clip flat. Turn sole to tie side and again stitch around sole, staying close to inside edge of bias binding. Hand-sew lauhala to bottom sole, using heavy thread.

This toddler's skirt, less full than the usual felt skirt, has decorations patterned after her own toys.

TOY APPLIQUÉS ON COVERALLS OR SKIRT

A felt skirt trimmed with gay pictures of her own toys makes a very personal garment for a little girl. This felt skirt is not made from the usual circle pattern which is relatively wasteful of material and tends to make any decorations hard to see because they are lost in the folds. Since felt needs no hemming, you can sew it fast.

A 26-inch square of felt is enough for a 3-year-old's skirt. To make a pattern, first measure the child's girth. Maximum distance around the entire skirt bottom can be about 48 inches. Divide the waist measurement by 4 and bottom measurement by 4. (For instance, a 20-inch waist — 5 inches, a 48-inch bottom — 12 inches.) Using these two measurements (plus ¾ inch to allow for seams) draw a skirt panel like the one shown in the sketch, after you have determined the skirt *length*. Lay the paper pattern on the felt and cut 4 panels. Machine-sew panels together, leaving a 3-inch placket opening at one seam top.

For a waistband cut two 1-inch strips, one slightly narrower than the other. Make them long enough to overlap at the placket. Place the wider strip ½ inch below the waistline of the skirt, on the *wrong* side. Put the other strip over it, on the *right* side of the skirt and about ⅛ inch from the top of the wider strip. Machine-sew along both edges and trim with narrow rick-rack braid. Sew snap fasteners to the placket.

Cut four shoulder straps, two an inch wide and two slightly more narrow. When you measure for straps long enough to cross in the back, also add about 2 inches to allow you to lengthen the skirt. Most tiny children seem to shoot up faster in height than they expand in width. This "margin of safety" could mean another year of wear!

Center each narrow strip on a 1-inch strip and stitch narrow rick-rack along the edges. Sew one end of each strap to the front of the skirt between the center and side seams; fasten the other ends to back with snap fasteners.

Add a small pocket edged in rick-rack. Make simple drawings of the child's favorite toys. Cut out drawings to use as patterns. Trace patterns on contrasting colorful scraps of felt which are available for 15 cents up in many fabric stores and hobby shops. Arrange the toy decorations in a band around the skirt bottom, between double rows of rick-rack. If you wish, glue the pieces to the skirt. Embroider in details and sew on beads and sequins.

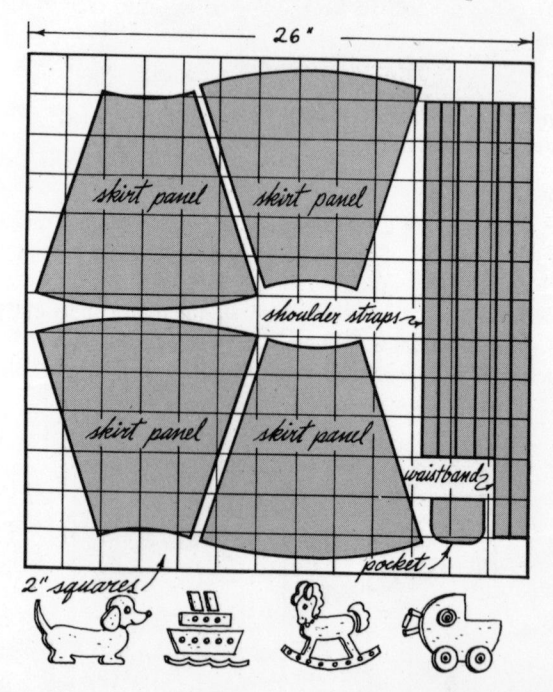

Sketch shows how to lay out skirt panel pattern, waistband, straps, and pocket on 26-inch square. Small drawings are sample toy decorations; use felt scraps.

The child in the photograph at right enjoys her gingerbread man appliquéd overalls all the more because they make her a "twin" to her cloth gingerbread dolls. You can put the rick-rack trim on a pair of plain, ready-made overalls, or you may prefer to make them out of the same material as used for the dolls.

To make the gingerbread dolls, you will need a yard of 36-inch chocolate brown Indian head cloth and the following notions (list includes materials for the gingerbread boy on the overalls): 8 yards of white rick-rack and about 2 yards of colored rick-rack, 1 skein each of white and pink 6-strand embroidery cotton, and an assortment of white buttons.

Cut a paper pattern for each doll. Cut the yard of fabric into 4 pieces, each 18 inches square. Fold two of the pieces in half, right side in, and place a pattern on each piece. Trace around the patterns with a soft pencil. Cut the front and back pieces for each doll at the same time, adding ½ inch for seams.

Now add the decorations and features. Pin white rick-rack around the edge of the front piece for each doll, and tack or machine-stitch in place. Use the colored rick-rack to detail the dress and jacket (see photo below).

Sew buttons in a row down the girl's dress and the boy's jacket. Embroider hair with the white cotton and outline a mouth with the pink. Make two large French knots for the nose. Sew on large white buttons for the eyes, using thread of a contrasting color. Add several buttons with solid tops for teeth.

With the right sides of the front and back pieces together, sew the girl doll together on the penciled line.

A gingerbread boy appliquéd on the front of this little girl's overalls matches her two gingerbread dolls.

Leave an opening of several inches, so you will be able to stuff the doll. Clip the seam allowance at right angles to the stitching in several places on each curve. Sew the two pieces in the same way for the boy doll.

Turn the dolls right side out and fill each with shredded foam rubber or kapok. Poke stuffing tightly into the hands and feet. Handstitch the holes closed.

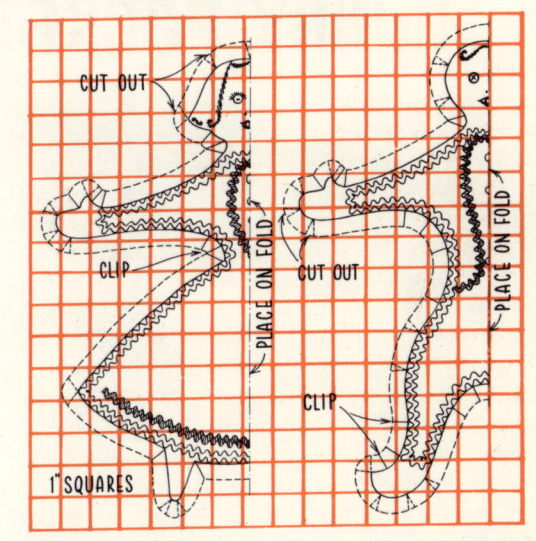

Make paper patterns exact size of half of finished doll. Add ½-inch seam allowance as you cut out the material.

Use your paper pattern of the boy doll as a guide for appliquéing the rick-rack on the child's overalls. Trace around the pattern lightly; then pin and sew white rick-rack over the penciled line. In the photograph at the top of page you see that a narrower rick-rack outlines a jacket with lapels. Add three small buttons for the eyes and nose, and a large red button for the mouth.

White rick-rack around dolls' edges gives the appearance of icing on a cake. Hair and mouth are outlined with embroidery cotton. Add buttons for eyes, vest, dress.

When pocket flap is up, smock's rabbit pocket shows a wide-awake expression. When pocket flap is down, as on the bear smock, sleepy fringe eyelashes cover the eyes.

SMOCK WITH A BUNNY POCKET

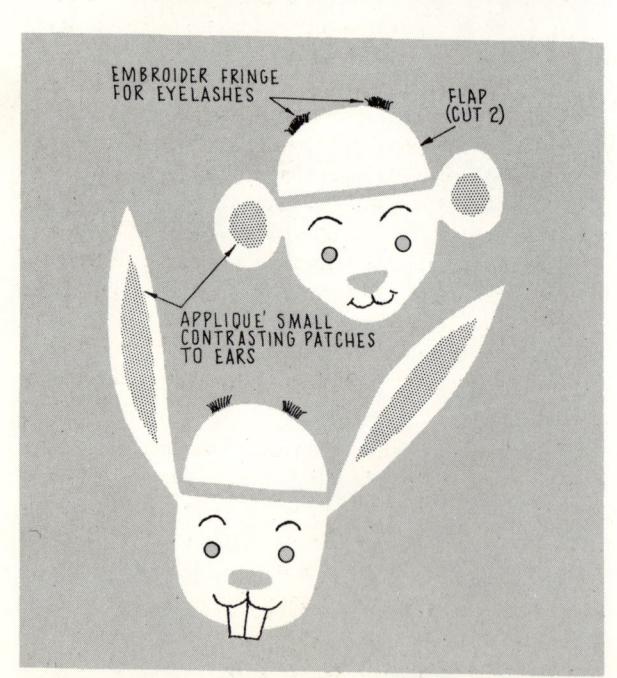

Sew on buttons for eyes, a bell for nose; embroider mouth, eyelashes. Use colorfast embroidery cotton. Be sure the "sleepy" flap completely covers the open eyes.

The child you like to sew for may not be easily lured into the practical cover-up of a smock. But we'll wager this

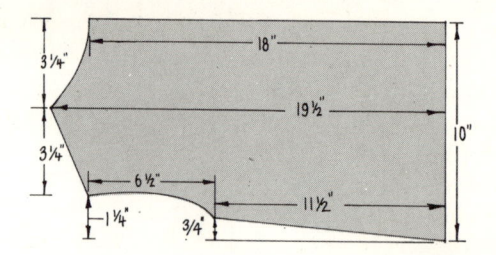

Lay pattern for front on fold of fabric; for back an inch from selvages to fold back for buttoning. Press back two long edges ½ inch, stitch, and press back again.

sleepy-time face — lift the flap to wake it up — is intriguing enough to do the trick. Your gamble is a morning's work and less than a yard of fabric. (Or you can appliqué the pocket to any suitable garment.)

Do the embroidery and appliqué the "inner ears" while the pocket is still unattached. Make the fringe eyelashes on the flap after facing it. Attach the pocket to the garment in the standard way (turn under edges, press, topstitch) or with the sewing machine's zigzag attachment. If you are making the rabbit, put on ears first, then the flaps, then the pocket.

THE SIMPLEST OF SMOCKS

Dimensions in upper plan are for a generous size 6. For another size, make your own pattern by measuring the

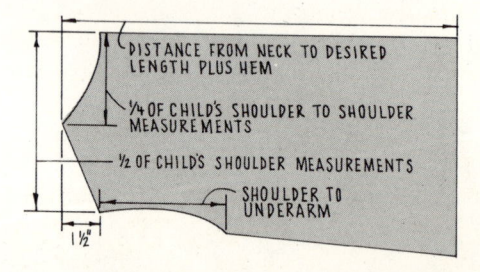

Distance across shoulders is basic to pattern. This measurement is divided, as shown, for neck, shoulder lengths. Armhole is half of entire shoulder measurement.

child and plotting the measurements on paper in the manner shown in the sketches. Although perfect fit is not crucial to this smock, be sure to make all measurements ample. To draw the shoulder angle, use one of the child's garments as a pattern.

Sew together seams, press open. Sew buttons on reinforced back opening. Bind neck and armholes with bias tape and decorate with rick-rack.

TRIM A SWEATER
...WITH COLORFUL FELT

Put a gaily decorated trim on a plain cardigan sweater and give a young girl a feeling of elegance. Appropriate for girls from 10 years old into their teens, these sweaters are a fancy addition to a special occasion wardrobe.

You appliqué sequins, beads, and metallic thread to a foundation piece of white felt which is tacked to the front of the sweater and around the neck opening.

To make a pattern for the collar section, fold the cardigan in half down the center of the back and lay sweater fold on the fold of a doubled piece of wrapping paper. Trace neck curve and continue the line along the front edge of sweater for 3½ inches. Remove sweater; trace another curve 3½ inches below the neck curve and parallel to it. These two curves form the collar pattern. Cut it out, trim away ½ inch from the top edge and pin the pattern around the neck opening of the sweater, ½ inch from the edge.

Next, cut two 2-inch wide strips of paper the length you want the decoration to extend down the front; lay them in place next to buttons and buttonholes. Tape strips to collar pattern. (Use pattern as a guide for amount of felt to buy.)

Trace basic pattern on another piece of paper before you begin to cut felt for one of the special patterns below. This will help you to plan the extra pieces of felt that you might want to set on to the foundation piece.

- *Clubs pattern:* Sweater in upper right photo has scalloped edges and continuous pieces of peacock blue felt stitched onto the white felt along both sides of the sweater and around the neck. The neck decoration — a series of shapes like playing card clubs — is from a separate pattern. (See sketch.) Sew a gold sequin in the center of each club and a pearl between each two figures. You may wish to outline both white and blue felt with gold thread.
- *Strawberry pattern:* This design has straight edges with 1/16-inch green rick-rack looped like a vine from strawberry to strawberry (bright red emery bags). Clusters of green felt leaves are appliquéd along the rick-rack with several white pearl buttons in between the groups of leaves. Gold braid trims inside edge.
- *Rick-rack pattern:* You'll need these materials to decorate a sweater like the one in the upper left of photo: a foundation piece of white felt; a small scrap of chartreuse felt; gold, red, yellow, turquoise, and black rick-rack; white buttons and gold thread.

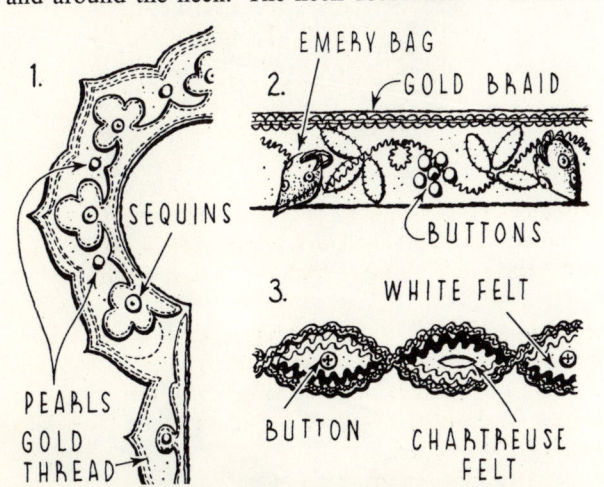

Place the braid on the white felt so each color forms a loose spiral, with turquoise and black pieces paralleling each other and the gold, red, and yellow pieces curving in the opposite direction. Tack rick-rack to felt with household cement to hold it while you sew.

In the center of every other rick-rack oval, cut out a small hole and back the hole with a piece of chartreuse felt. Sew a white button in centers of alternate ovals. Trim away white felt around outside edges of rick-rack.

Sew the decorated white foundation felt strips to the cardigan quite loosely — sweater will stretch when put on.

OLD LACE

Old lace adds a quaint touch to a sweater. Sew it on loosely, leaving ample slack between the contact points so thread will not break when sweater is worn. For added color, thread the lace with ribbon. Antique lace by dipping it for a few minutes in coffee or tea.

Strawberries on lower left sweater are bright red emery bags sewn on green felt vine. Peacock blue scallops on upper right sweater. Multi-colored rick-rack ovals decorate the sweater at upper left.

Sketches of part of each sweater decoration showing details of: (1) Clubs, (2) Strawberry, and (3) Rick-rack.

This monkey, made of men's work-weight cotton socks, looks as if he is wearing little white socks and gloves.

TO MAKE A MONKEY

For the child who likes to keep a menagerie, you can make this monkey from one pair of men's heavy cotton work socks — preferably the mottled grey type with white

If one monkey on a high wire is good, two monkeys are better. Note vests and caps, made from bright remnants.

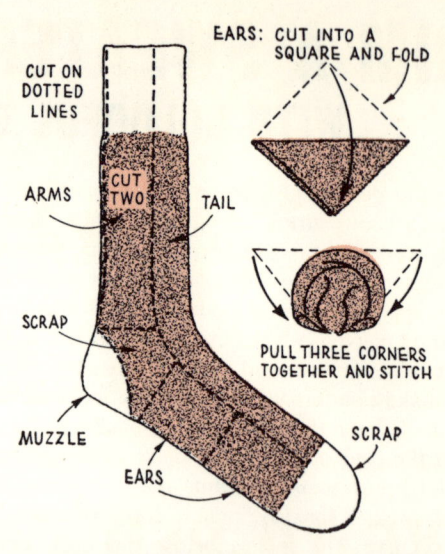

heels, toes, and tops. One sock becomes head, body, and legs. The other sock is cut up into arms, tail, muzzle, and ears. The eyes are buttons and the mouth is red stitching.

Follow directions given in the sketches. After you stuff the body, then fill arms and tail. Sew these, and also the muzzle and ears to the body and head.

The little cap and coat shown on the monkeys here could be made from gay colored remnants or a child's bright sock.

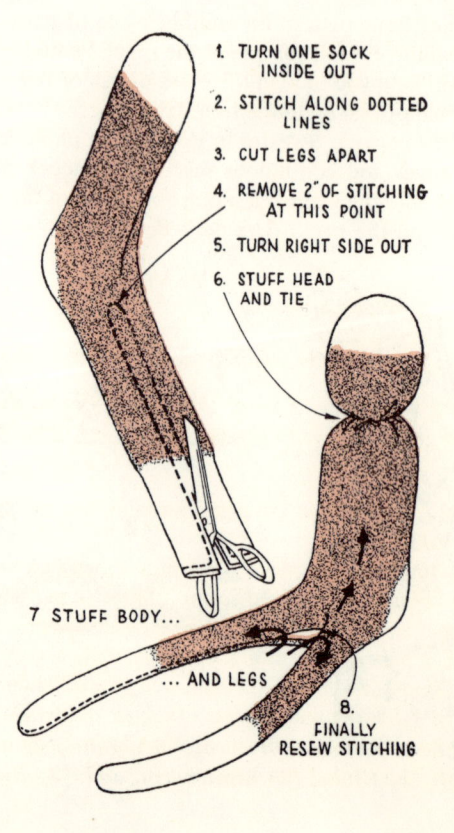

EARS: CUT INTO A SQUARE AND FOLD

CUT ON DOTTED LINES

ARMS — CUT TWO — TAIL

SCRAP

PULL THREE CORNERS TOGETHER AND STITCH

MUZZLE

EARS

SCRAP

1. TURN ONE SOCK INSIDE OUT
2. STITCH ALONG DOTTED LINES
3. CUT LEGS APART
4. REMOVE 2" OF STITCHING AT THIS POINT
5. TURN RIGHT SIDE OUT
6. STUFF HEAD AND TIE
7. STUFF BODY... ...AND LEGS
8. FINALLY RESEW STITCHING

Children may use cat, turtle, or fish as pillows or as toys. Stuff with foam rubber, shredded or slab-type.

TAKE-TO-BED PILLOW TOYS

The three stuffed toys shown above are multi-purpose. They not only whittle down your stack of fabric scraps but they appeal to a wide age group as bed decorations or toys.

FISH
Make a paper pattern and trace its outline on an inch wide (or narrower) slab of foam rubber or polyurethane foam. After you cut out the filling, cut two fabric cover pieces

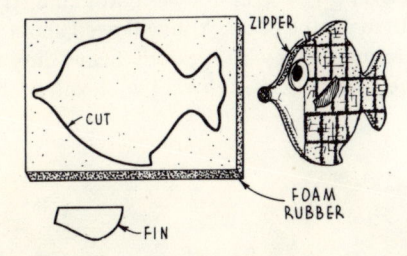

Fish toy is filled with foam slab cut to shape. You may wish to add a zipper to the cover for easy removal.

an inch or two larger (to accommodate the thickness of the foam).

Machine-sew the pieces together, leaving an unsewed section where you can slip in the filling. If you like, sew in a zipper so the cover can be removed easily for washing.

Cut a pair of fins and face them with a contrasting fabric. Hand-sew fins to the fish, one on each side. Make a pair of felt eyes and a nose. Tack in place. For extra design interest, make most of the fish's body from a printed material and the head of plain fabric.

TURTLE
Cut two large, plate-sized circles of fabric and two strips twice as long as the circumference of the circle. One circle and one strip (the pieces that will be on top to form the "shell") could be printed and the rest of the turtle plain. Cut curves at ends of ruffle pieces so that where they meet they will not obscure the turtle's head. Face the figured strip with the plain material and gather into a ruffle.

Cut and sew together the pieces for the legs and the tail. Stuff these little sacks with shredded foam. Machine-

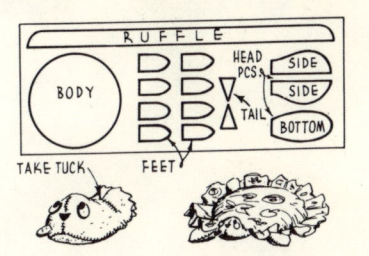

Make turtle's "shell" of gay printed fabric. Cut the remaining pieces from plain material.

sew together the top circle, the ruffle, the legs, and bottom circle, leaving an opening for the turtle's head.

Cut head (see sketch). Take a few tucks to shape it. Stuff, and sew on felt eyes, nose, and tongue. Stuff the round pillow and insert the head. Hand-sew body.

CAT
After cutting cat's body, cut out legs, arms, head, and ears. The front pieces might be of a plain color and the back a patterned material. Sew together the front and back pieces of legs, arms, and ears. Stuff with shredded foam.

To make the cat's head, take tucks along the cheeks and forehead. Embroider a face and then sew ears to one

Cut two of each of the pieces shown in the sketch above. Pinafore, sketched on cat with dotted lines, is optional.

of the head pieces. Sew the two head pieces together and stuff. Sew all of the small stuffed pieces and the head to one of the body pieces. Sew back and front of the cat together, leaving an opening to stuff body. Hand-stitch to close, and dress in a simple pinafore.

87

Floppy yet sturdy yarn animals are just the sort of toys children love. They are perfect for take-to-bed toys.

HOW TO MAKE YARN ANIMALS

Somehow, fluffy yarn animals seem to be "grandmother specialties" because they are the cuddly sort of toy grandmothers like to give their grandchildren. Each of the little animals above is soft, yet sturdy enough to withstand tugging.

Each animal is made of 7 pieces: a body, 4 legs, a head, and a tail. You wrap the yarn around a rectangular template to make the parts. You will need about 3 ounces of 4-ply Germantown yarn for each, heavy duty thread, a tapestry needle, buttons, felt scraps, a knife, and heavy

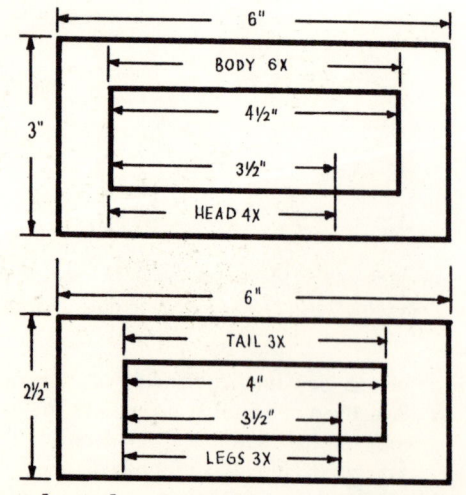

1. Scratch numbers in two plastic templates with a pin.

2. Wrap yarn loosely around template between the lines.

3. Back-stitch yarn down center with heavy duty thread.

4. Cut yarn free, then fluff piece into a sausage shape.

cardboard or a ⅛-inch sheet of plastic for the template.

(Plastic templates are more durable than cardboard and will not buckle. Buy sheet plastic at a hobby shop and cut out the two templates with a jig saw or coping saw, using dimensions in the sketch.)

The numbers in the sketch show you where and how many times to fill the template for each main piece—4 times for the head, 3 times for the tail, and so forth. (The "x" means times.) Wrap only a single layer of yarn at a time, and firm the strands close together.

If you wish, make an animal with paws of a different color from the rest of the body. When you make the legs, wrap ¾ of the leg template the required number of times with body color, then wrap the rest of the template with the paw color. Be sure to start at the paw end when you sew the yarn.

Next, using a back stitch, sew across the center of the yarn with heavy duty thread. When you back stitch, you push the needle through the yarn ahead of the sewing, and then re-insert it so that it overlaps the last stitch slightly. Stitched this way, all strands of yarn will be held by the thread. Leave a length of thread about 5 inches long when you finish.

Now, cut the yarn away from the template by drawing a knife along each of the wrapped edges. Hold the yarn by the tail of thread and beat it lightly against your knee. This will make the yarn fluff out into a sausage shape.

To make an animal with a muzzle like the lion's, wrap the yarn for the head on a *cardboard* template. After you sew the yarn, cut the template open at one end, and slip the yarn off instead of cutting it. Sew the two ends together and cut all the loops except those in the center of the head that make the muzzle. Fluff out the yarn.

Make all 7 pieces the same way. Sew the ends of the head piece together and join the various parts in proper position on the body. Be sure to sew through the stitching at center of each piece rather than just through the yarn.

Embroider nose and mouth. Use colored buttons for eyes. For whiskers pull two double strands of yarn through nose. Cut ears and tongue from scraps of felt.

5. Sew parts of body together; stitch firmly in center.

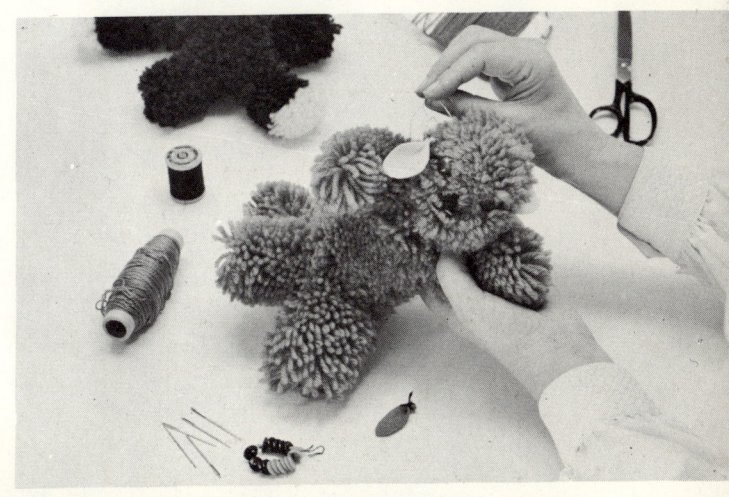

6. Ears, tongue cut extra long as part is hidden in yarn.

89

PUPPETS
A SMALL HANDFUL OF SHOW BUSINESS

You could easily inspire a whole collection of these sock and glove puppets by giving a child just a few. Any youngster who can sew on a button will have his own ideas about the creatures he'll want to create for himself. These make fine birthday party entertainers, and you might also allow your child to help you make them for friends or cousins on his gift list.

A large part of these puppets' charm is their simplicity. One stocking or glove serves as both body and head. You add only enough details to highlight each puppet's particular character. You'll find your imagination being guided by the sock or glove itself. For example, a green argyle sock was turned into the "diamondback" snake in the photograph below. A discarded red glove became the Indian on the opposite page.

To make these puppets you'll need an assortment of buttons, a needle and thread, and several odd mittens, gloves, and men's or boys' socks. You'll also find surprising and clever uses for bits of felt, cloth binding tape that can be ironed on, upholstery fringe, pipe cleaners, yarn, and ribbon.

FOUR BASIC METHODS

Here are basic ways to make a hand puppet. Your choice depends on the anatomy of the creature the puppet is supposed to represent:

1. If the animal's muzzle is a prominent feature, as it is on a bloodhound for example, use the heel of the sock as the puppet's nose. When the puppeteer puts his hand inside, he can extend the nose with his thumb and make it move freely by moving his thumb back and forth. Make a bloodhound's ears with the toe sections of a pair of socks.

2. For a puppet whose nose is fairly important, or when you want the puppet to have a mouth that can open and close, fold the bulge of the heel to the inside and stitch the edges of the fold together so the body of the sock is a straight cylinder down to the toe. Slit the material at the toe and insert a piece of felt, as shown in the giraffe sketch. If you paint the giraffe's spots with textile paint, you can put him in the wash when he gets dirty.

To make this puppet talk, place your thumb under the mouth and your fingers above it. You might also make an

With a sock puppet on his hand — presto! — a child becomes a showman. In drama below: a snake, Santa, a cat.

Like a balloon, a puppet comes close to being a universal toy, knowing no age boundary and providing instant fun for both boys and girls. Had Winnie the Pooh had his mind on puppets instead of balloons at the time, he might have said, "Nobody can be uncheered by a puppet."

- FIST PUPPETS made from socks, gloves.
- WINNIE THE POOH and friends — all on strings...
- FINGER PUPPETS so small that they can perform in a windowed grocery carton.
- PUPPET STAGE for home theatricals.

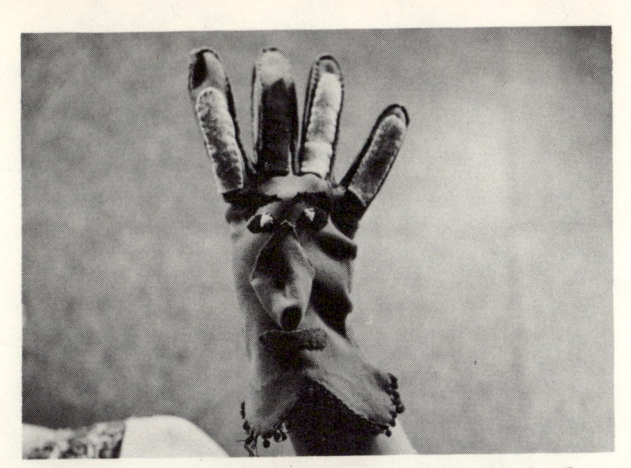

Felt-covered fingers of old red glove are Indian feathers. Transplant glove thumb to face center for nose.

elephant this way. Add rolls of crinoline or white nylon net for the elephant's tusks and sew a narrow piece from the other sock around more crinoline and a pipe cleaner to make a trunk.

3. For a very simple sock puppet — perhaps for a young child with a small hand — make a V-shaped cut at the heel of the sock and remove the toe section. Stitch the pointed pieces together for ears, and add button eyes and scraps of felt for other features. You make this puppet move by inserting two fingers in each ear.

4. Twin puppets — one for each hand, or one each for a small brother and sister — are made from a pair of wool mittens. They have button eyes with fringe eyelashes, felt ears, and many loops of yarn for hair. The mitten thumb is sewn to form a pouting mouth.

You can give special expressions to the puppet's eyes by using buttons of an unusual shape or color. Try sewing the button eyes over larger round pieces of felt, or sew curved pieces of felt above the button for eyebrows. Other possible accessories are padded ears, twigs for a reindeer's antlers, drapery fringe for a beard or mane, braided yarn for hair, or a small felt hat.

SIMPLE STAGE

Children may use these puppets with or without a stage. Although most children enjoy giving "a real puppet play," a child often likes to carry a puppet in his pocket to pull out for an impromptu performance, or just when he feels the need to "talk to someone."

An impromptu stage may be set up in a few minutes merely by pinning a folded sheet over two backs of chairs which are placed the length of the sheet apart. Puppeteers

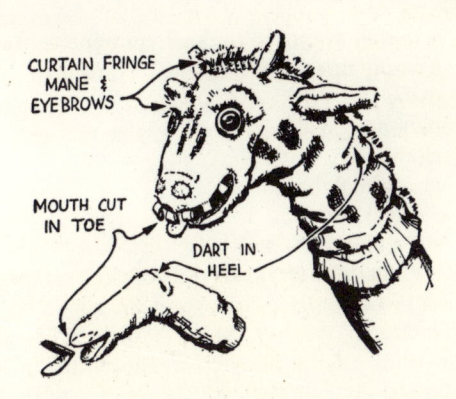

Pouting twin puppets with curly yarn hair were woolen mittens. They have button eyes and pink felt ears.

Giraffe has felt mouth, tongue sewn into toe of sock.

work behind the scenes, hold their puppets above the sheet for the action. The chair seats are handy for props.

Another possibility is to cut a door-width piece of heavy cardboard (one side of a huge cardboard carton). Make it just a little higher than a child and cut an ample opening for the puppets' action at a height where children can kneel and manipulate their puppets. A hall doorway is ideal for this — puppeteers on hall side, audience in the other room.

"Winnie the Pooh" on strings! Owl is stuffed but Piglet and Pooh are variations of method described here.

Miniature stage props, like Pooh's famous honey bucket, can be carved from scraps of balsa. They add reality.

"WINNIE THE POOH" MARIONETTES

Winnie the Pooh, Piglet, Owl, Eeyore, and all the inhabitants of "100 Aker Wood" have been children's friends for several generations — and these appealing little marionettes will make them even more real to your children.

Simple enough for even a very young child to manipulate, these small string puppets can be made with a skeleton of spools and a ping-pong ball for a head.

The materials you need for each marionette are:
- 6 empty thread spools (all 125-yard size)
- twine
- ping-pong ball
- cloth
- needle and thread
- 3/8-inch doweling
- strong black thread
- buttons, pipe cleaners, yarn, oilcloth scraps

With a piece of string, tie two of the spools together about an inch apart, so they can move freely. These spools form the trunk of the body. Thread another piece of string 11 inches long through the hole in each of the trunk spools and tie the 4 remaining spools to the 4 ends. (See sketch, lower left.) These make the puppet's legs (if he's an animal), or arms and legs (if he's not).

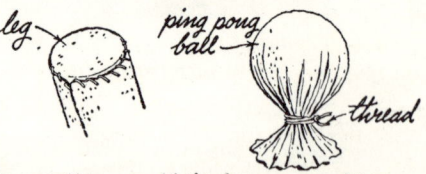

Make a pattern on 1/2-inch square grid paper. Place the pattern on a double thickness of the cloth you have chosen for the body; cut. You will have less sewing to do if the longest edge is on a fold. Sew the pieces together about 1/4 inch from the edge. Do not sew across the bottom of each foot. Also, leave an opening to the neck.

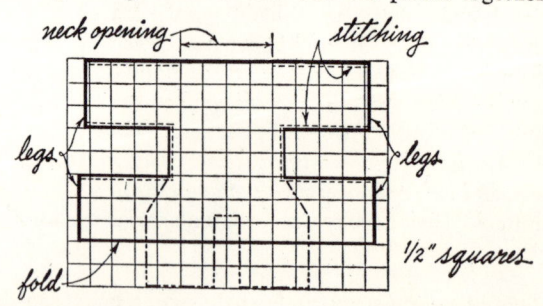

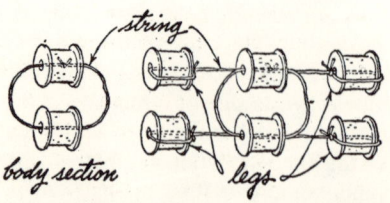

Marionettes are flexible, easy to manipulate, yet sturdy because spool joints are loosely tied with string.

MAKING THE BODY

Turn the covering inside out through the neck hole so your sewing is inside. Insert the spools, one at a time, through the neck opening. Start with the back legs and work spools into place inside the body.

Now cut 4 pieces of material in 1 1/2-inch squares. These are for the bottoms of the feet. Place one of the squares over the end of the spool in each leg opening. With a pencil, work the material up around the spool inside each leg. With the foot piece taut over the spool end, fold under edges of body piece and stitch it and foot together.

THE HEAD AND FACE

Cut a 6-inch square of material for the head. Put the ball in the center and gather the corners together. Pull the cloth tightly around ball, distributing the extra fullness into a number of little tucks. Then wrap thread several times around corners and tie. Trim loose end of material close to the thread. Insert edges of head piece into the neck opening and sew together securely.

The marionette is now ready for his face features. Just what you add depends on what kind of a character you want the puppet to be. Buttons or circles of oilcloth make good eyes. Pipe cleaners are fine for noses and tails, and yarn may be used for mañes. Ears can be fashioned from the same material as the rest of the body.

In the case of Eeyore, Winnie the Pooh's donkey friend in the upper right photo on the opposite page, a thimble was glued to the ping-pong ball inside his head to form a jaw. Pooh's nose is stuffed with kapok. Variations of the basic pattern could include a long neck to make a giraffe; or an enlargement of the pattern and spools to make an elephant.

STRINGING THE MARIONETTE

For strings to work the puppet, cut two pieces of black linen thread 2 feet long. Attach one piece to back of puppet's head and the other to the cloth at the base of the tail. Tie the free ends of thread to a 7-inch length of doweling. Add more strings if you want to control the arms of a puppet like Pooh in the pictures. Attach the arm strings to a separate dowel.

Tangled strings are one of the few troubles your child could have with this puppet. When it is ready to be put away, hold the doweling so the puppet hangs free. Twist the strings by giving the puppet a twirl. Then wrap strings loosely around the doweling.

An armchair, with the seat as the stage and the back as a screen for the puppet master, has long been a favorite and seems especially appropriate.

A PUPPET TO FIT THE FIST

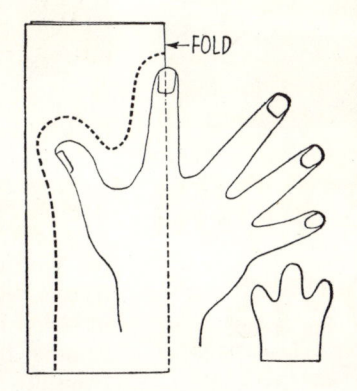

You are in for a store of fun when you and your children make this fist puppet. Use a child's hand as pattern guide to the body.

Put cloth, cotton, yarn, and buttons together into a puppet and watch it come to life on the hand of a small child!

Fist puppets are so simple. And here's how your children can help you in the making. Draw a pattern by tracing an *exaggerated* outline of the thumb and index finger of your child's hand on paper which has been folded in the middle. With the paper still folded, cut along the penciled outline so that both sides of the "glove" will be the same.

Place pattern on doubled fabric so that you will cut out two pieces. Sew these, right sides together, leaving only the bottom of the glove open. Turn glove to right side to hide the seams.

For the head use unbleached muslin. Cut out two circles, about 4 inches in diameter, and sew them together leaving a finger-sized hole in which to put the stuffing. Turn right side out and fill with kapok or cotton. Be sure to use enough to make the head firm.

Now, have your child put on the glove and let him push his finger up into the stuffed head. As he is supporting the puppet you carefully sew the edges of the head hole around the bottom of the index finger of the glove.

Let the children decide on the face and the hair. If they are over six, they probably can finish the puppet themselves. They can paint the face with textile paint and sew on hair of yarn, embroidery floss, or frayed rope.

Most productions need just two finger puppets at a time. Let the children make their own puppets — for their favorite stories — and their plays will have special appeal.

FINGER PUPPETS

Small children enjoy performing at home with these finger puppets as much as they delight in acting in school plays.

The stage is just a cardboard carton from the grocery store with its top cut off. It rests upside-down on four ¾-inch dowel legs, so the operator's arm will have ample room to move from below. Staple the legs up the inside edges of the box. Cut the stage opening from the front of the box with a sharp knife, and reinforce across the bottom with a glued-on piece of yardstick. Paint the inside of the box black, and cover the outside with burlap or other fabric. A cloth drape, stapled to the front and two sides, hides the stage legs and the operator's arm.

Bodies of the puppets are obtained from the pasteboard cones that are used as string bobbins, or from rolled-up and glued cones of construction paper. Paint them, or costume with cloth scraps. Adding small bells gives them a gay sound. Any household glue will hold the sequins, cotton hair, bead eyes, and hats.

Puppets can be quite simple or very elaborate. Black back of stage is decorated with gummed metallic stars.

Puppets' heads are styrene foam balls. Other materials are cloth scraps, pipe cleaners, cotton, sequins, tiny bells.

Several puppets can be operated on the fingers of one hand, although this requires some practice.

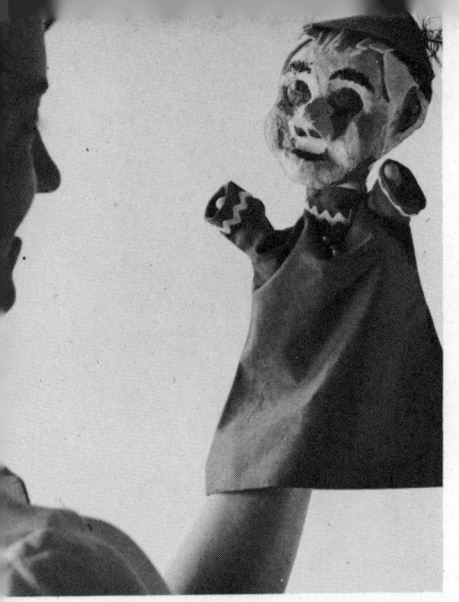

Puppeteer moves fingers to make puppet dance, fight, or clap.

1. To make head form, model soft clay around modeling stand or a small light globe.

2. Cover form with squares of paste-dampened paper towels.

FUN-TO-MAKE PUPPET

With adult supervision, a child of six or older can have fun creating the puppet pictured here.

First, form the puppet's head in soft modeling clay. Use either a modeling stand or a small light globe set in the top of a cardboard tube. Be sure to make an inch or more of neck. Dip finished clay head into melted paraffin and allow wax coating to harden. The wax permits easier removal, later on, of the papier mâché covering of the clay form.

Tear paper towels or newspapers into squares; soak them in creamy paste of flour and water cooked a few minutes and cooled. Mold the first layer of squares over the clay head. Continue to build up the layers of papier mâché until a strong shell is made. Smooth the edges and surface; allow to dry for at least 24 hours.

When the shell is dry, cut it in half (a front half and a back half) with a sharp knife. Slip off the waxed clay form. Hold the head halves together and carefully cover the slit with more patches of papier mâché. Dry for 24 hours.

Paint features with poster paint; add yarn wigs and beards; glue on cloth garment. The puppeteer's index finger fits into the neck of the puppet; thumb and middle finger fit into sleeves.

3. Build up strong shell with several layers of papier mâché.

4. Cut dry shell in half and slip off waxed mold. Glue halves together with papier mâché.

5. Decorate with crayons or poster paint. Add garment.

Puppet stage for that first experience with "live" theater. Behind-scenes action hidden from floor-level audience.

STAGE...
THEATER...
TICKET WINDOW

For your young children—and the whole neighborhood, too—build a stage for their favorite puppets.

The generous size of this stage allows two hidden puppeteers to operate fist puppets from the pit below or to manipulate string puppets from behind the backdrop. Bright cotton curtains, hung on a standard traverse rod, are dramatically drawn for the grand overture or exciting climax.

The little stage is complete and needs no special background or location. Light in weight, it can be moved to suit a prima donna's whims. Before the productions, it doubles as a ticket booth for the home theatricals.

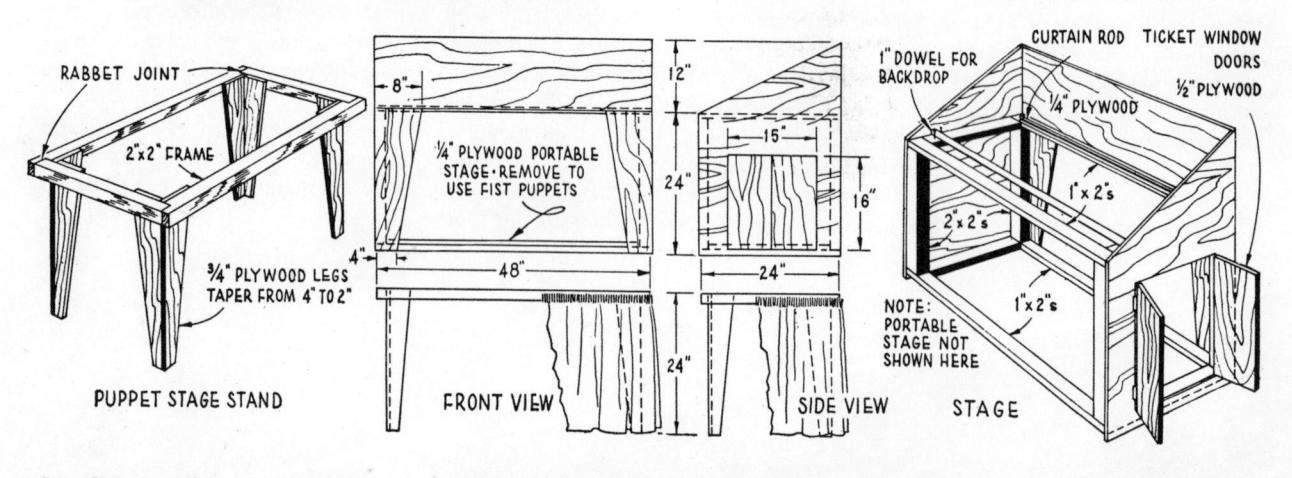

PUPPET STAGE STAND — RABBET JOINT, 2"x2" FRAME, ¾" PLYWOOD LEGS TAPER FROM 4" TO 2"

FRONT VIEW — 8", ¼" PLYWOOD PORTABLE STAGE·REMOVE TO USE FIST PUPPETS, 12", 24", 4", 48", 24"

SIDE VIEW — 15", 16", 24"

STAGE — CURTAIN ROD, TICKET WINDOW, 1" DOWEL FOR BACKDROP, DOORS ½" PLYWOOD, ¼" PLYWOOD, 1"x2"s, 2"x2"s, 1"x2"s, NOTE: PORTABLE STAGE NOT SHOWN HERE

Standing in line at the ticket window adds theatrical realism.

Removable stage is lifted out for fist puppets; operators sit on floor.

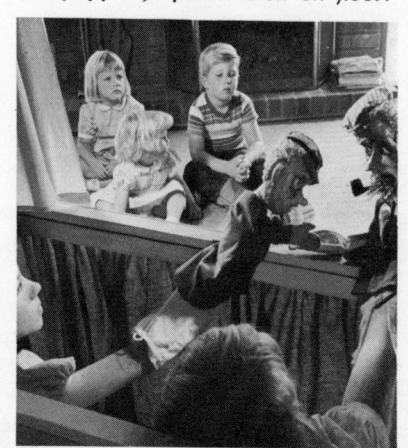

Operators stand on stools to work string puppets from above back rail.

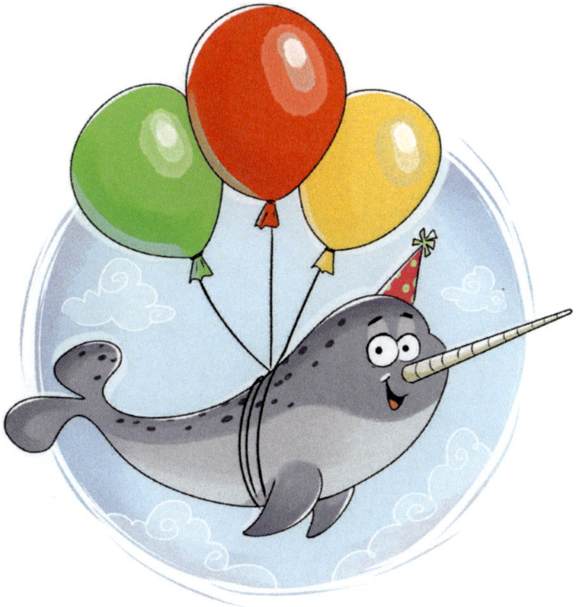

FOR ELI, ZEV, EZRA, & ARI –

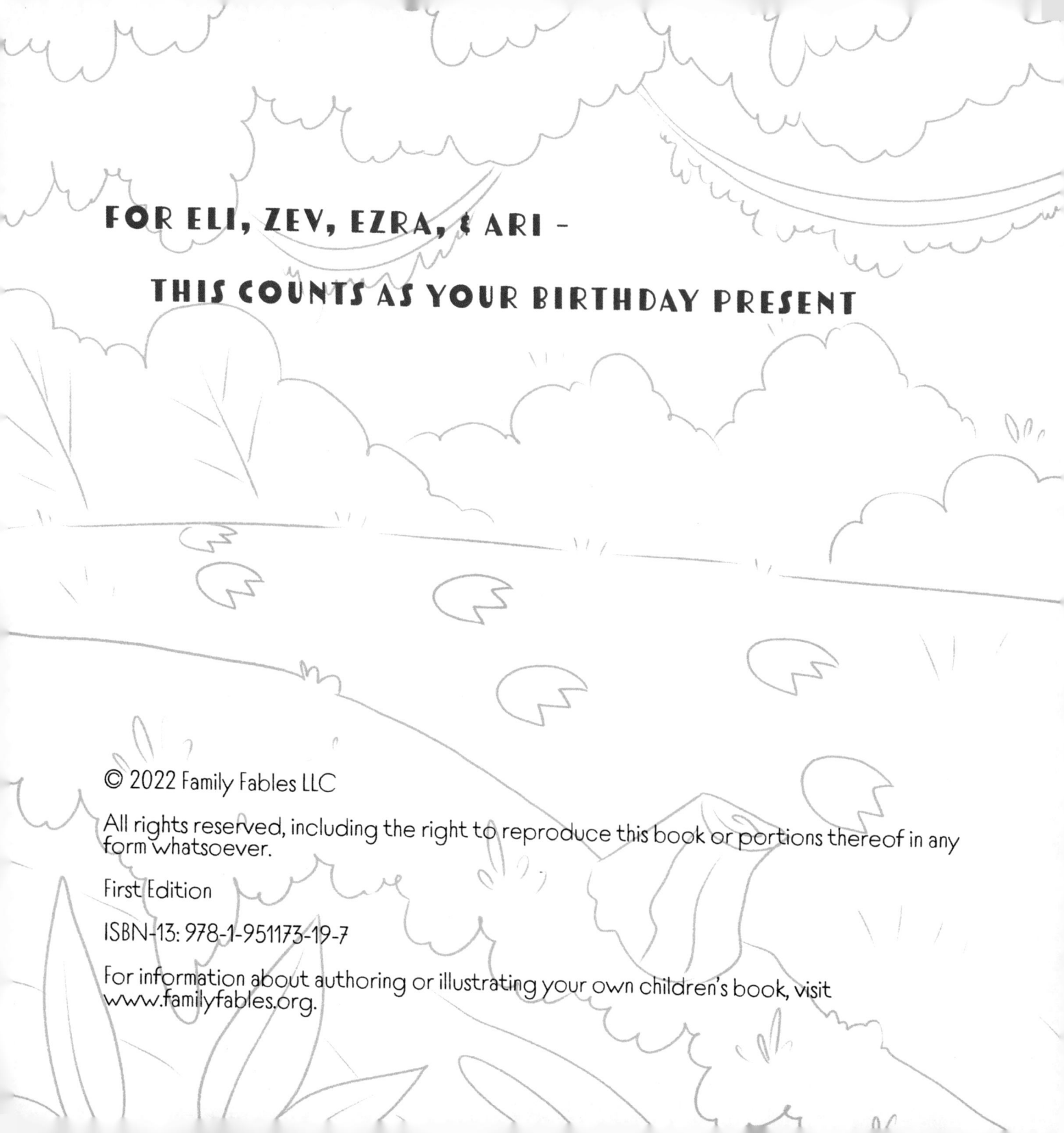

THIS COUNTS AS YOUR BIRTHDAY PRESENT

© 2022 Family Fables LLC

All rights reserved, including the right to reproduce this book or portions thereof in any form whatsoever.

First Edition

ISBN-13: 978-1-951173-19-7

For information about authoring or illustrating your own children's book, visit www.familyfables.org.

FINDING HAMPTON

a family fable

Story by: Z. P. Phillips   Art by: A. N. Serebrennikova

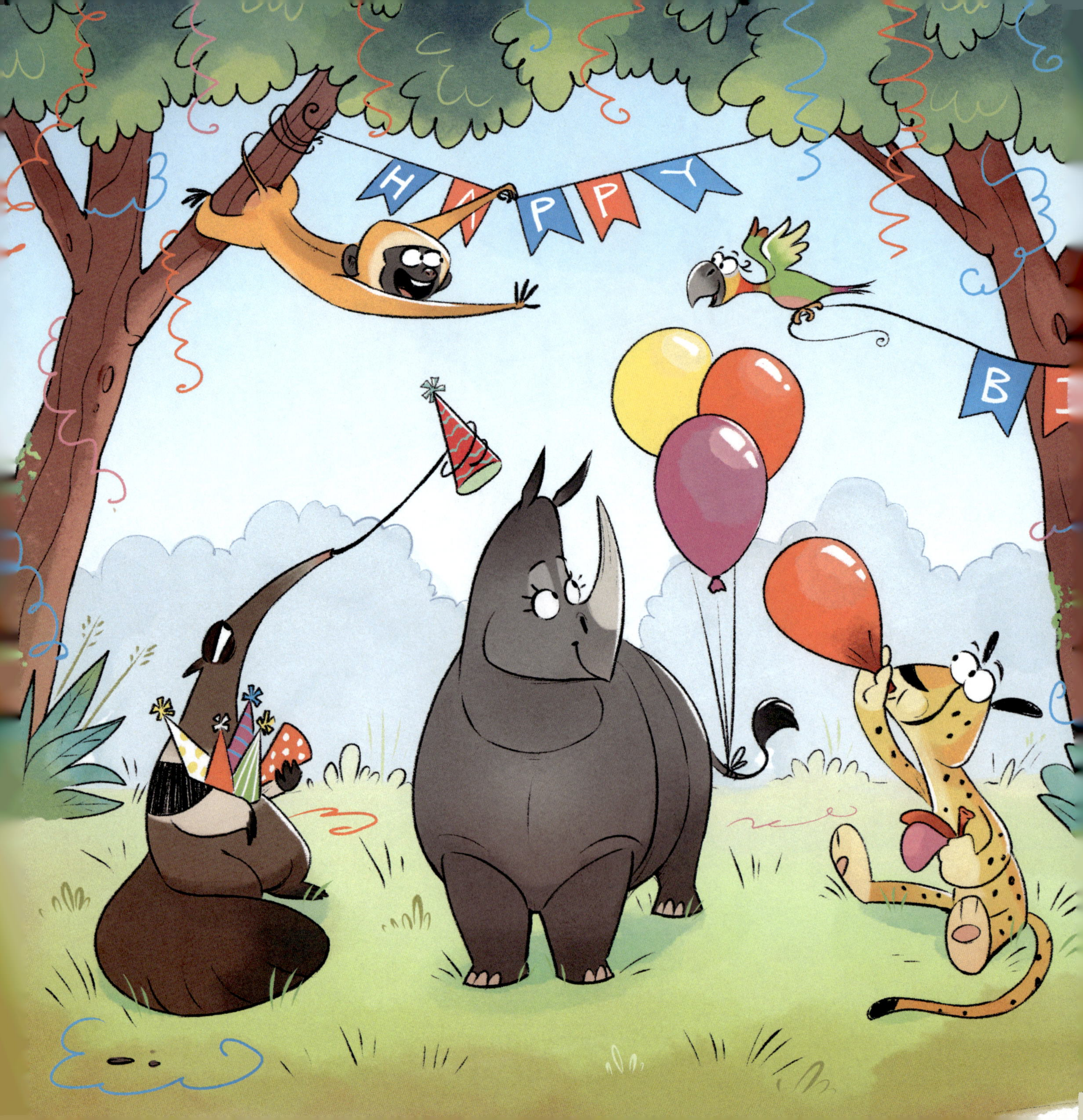
HAPPY
B

It was Rosie's birthday, and Hampton was in search of a gift for her.

A last minute gift.

He was very stressed.

What could Rosie want?!?

A fan?

Some worms?

A bubble bath?

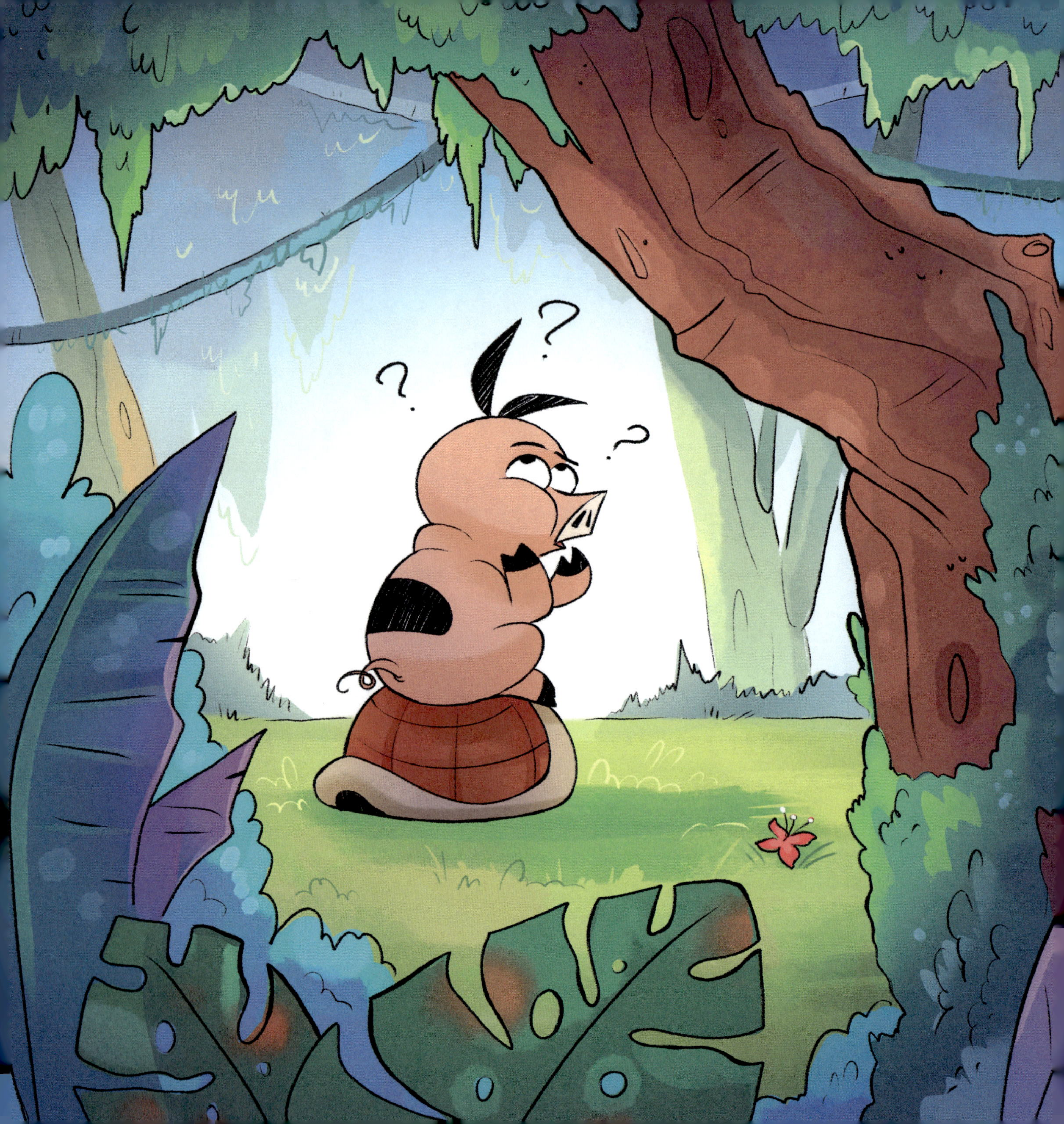

Hampton took a seat on a nearby rock so he could **REALLY** focus. He needed 100% of his brain power dedicated to birthday present thinking.

So, he thought.

And, he thought.

And, he thought.

Until he realized...
THE ROCK COULD WALK!

That's it!!!
A walking rock! Rhinos love rocks.
But a walking rock!?! It's perfect.

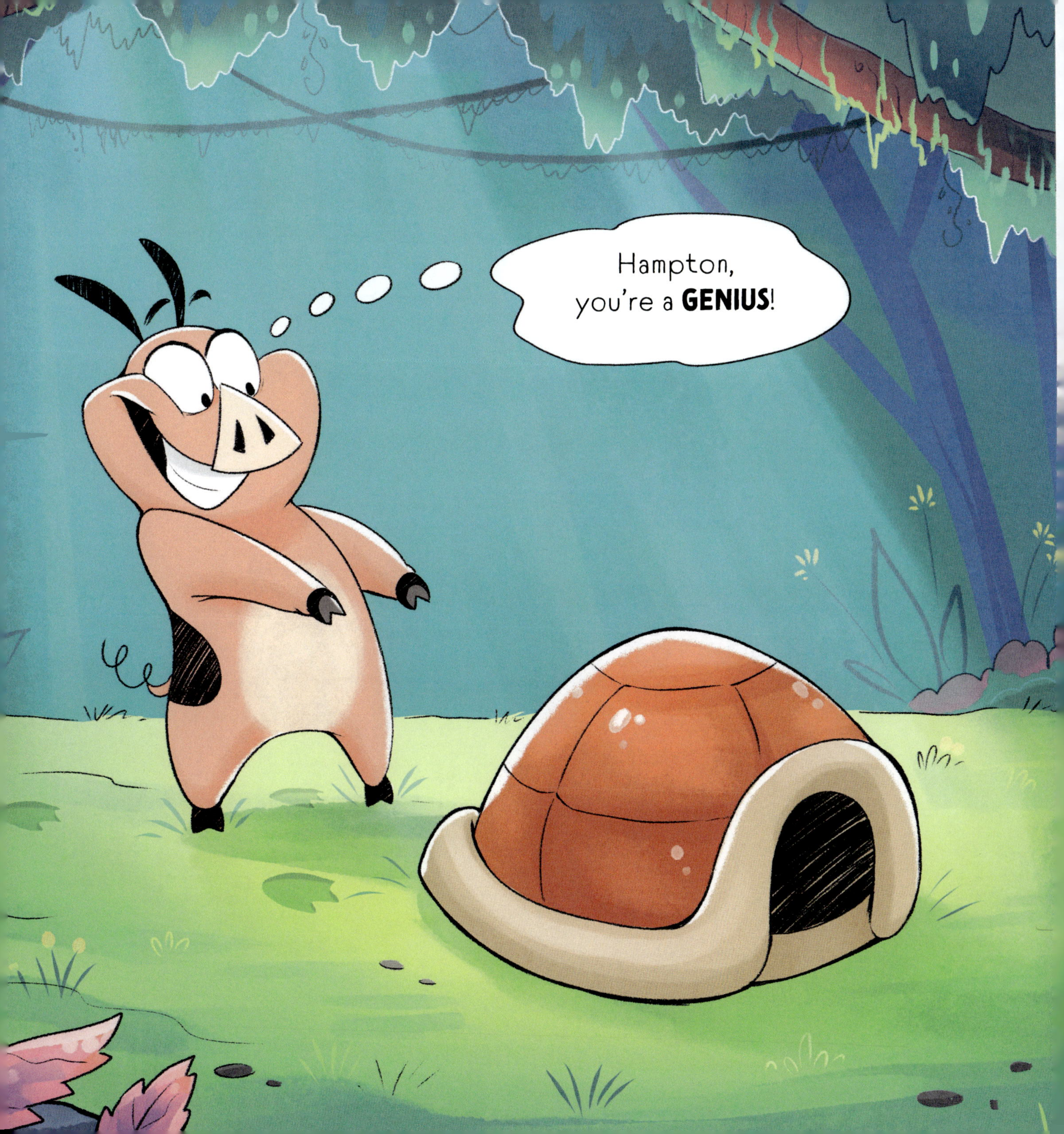
Hampton, you're a **GENIUS**!

Hampton reached to pick it up, but the rock took off!

Again.

And again.

And again.

Hampton spent hours tracking this elusive rock.

In fact, he walked so far and so long that he couldn't even hear his friends searching for him.

Using Hampton's special call, his friends yelled out at the top of their lungs:

Oink! Oink!

snort *snort*

Piggy! Piggy!

Up trees.

Oink! Oink!

snort *snort*

Piggy! Piggy!

In the water.

Oink! Oink! *snort* *snort* Piggy! Piggy!

In the grass.

In bananas.

In anthills.

In the sky.

Under Rosie.

Not

hing.

Hampton was too far and too focused on tracking this rock.

Just then, he got a pig-of-a-genius idea!

POUNCE!

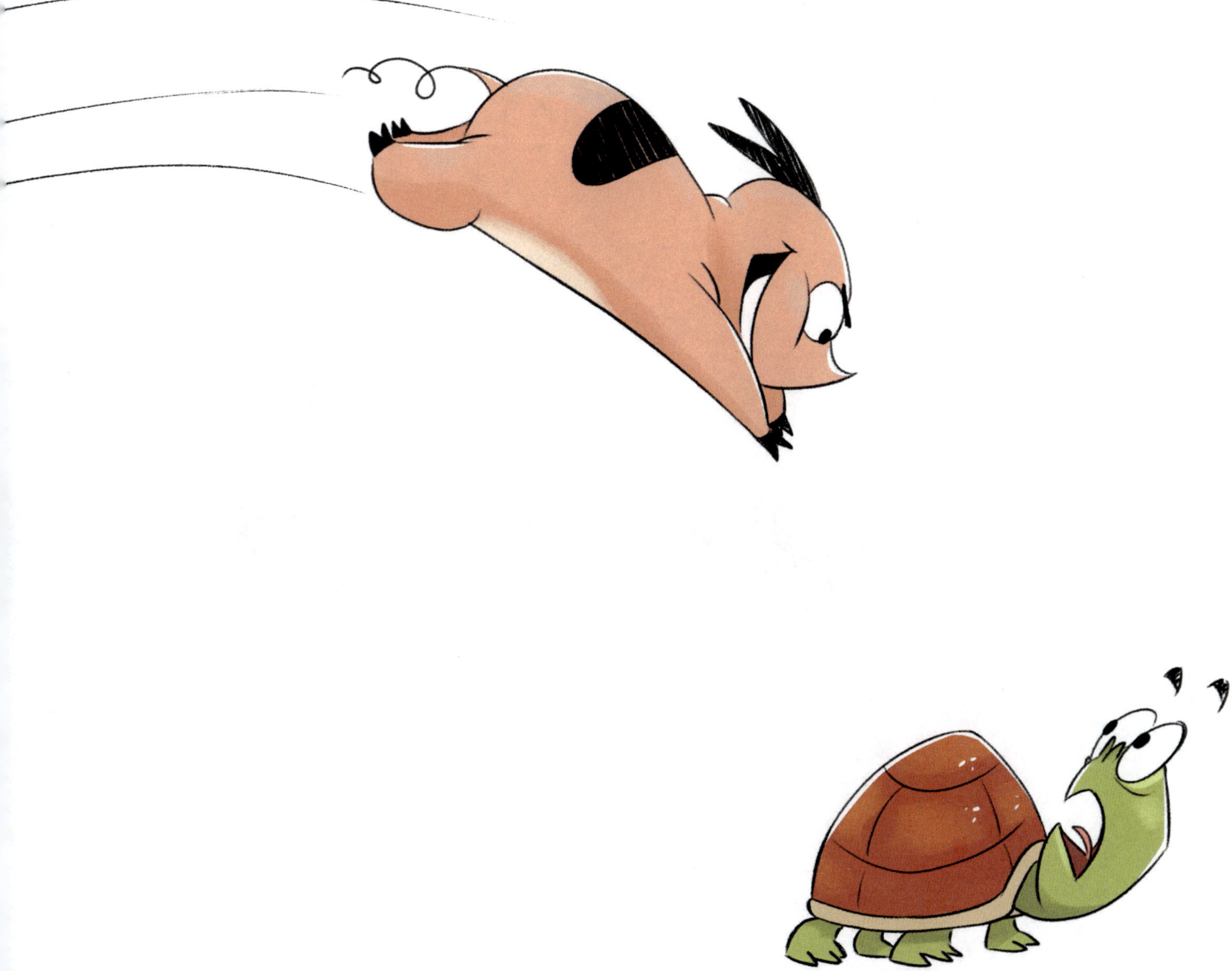

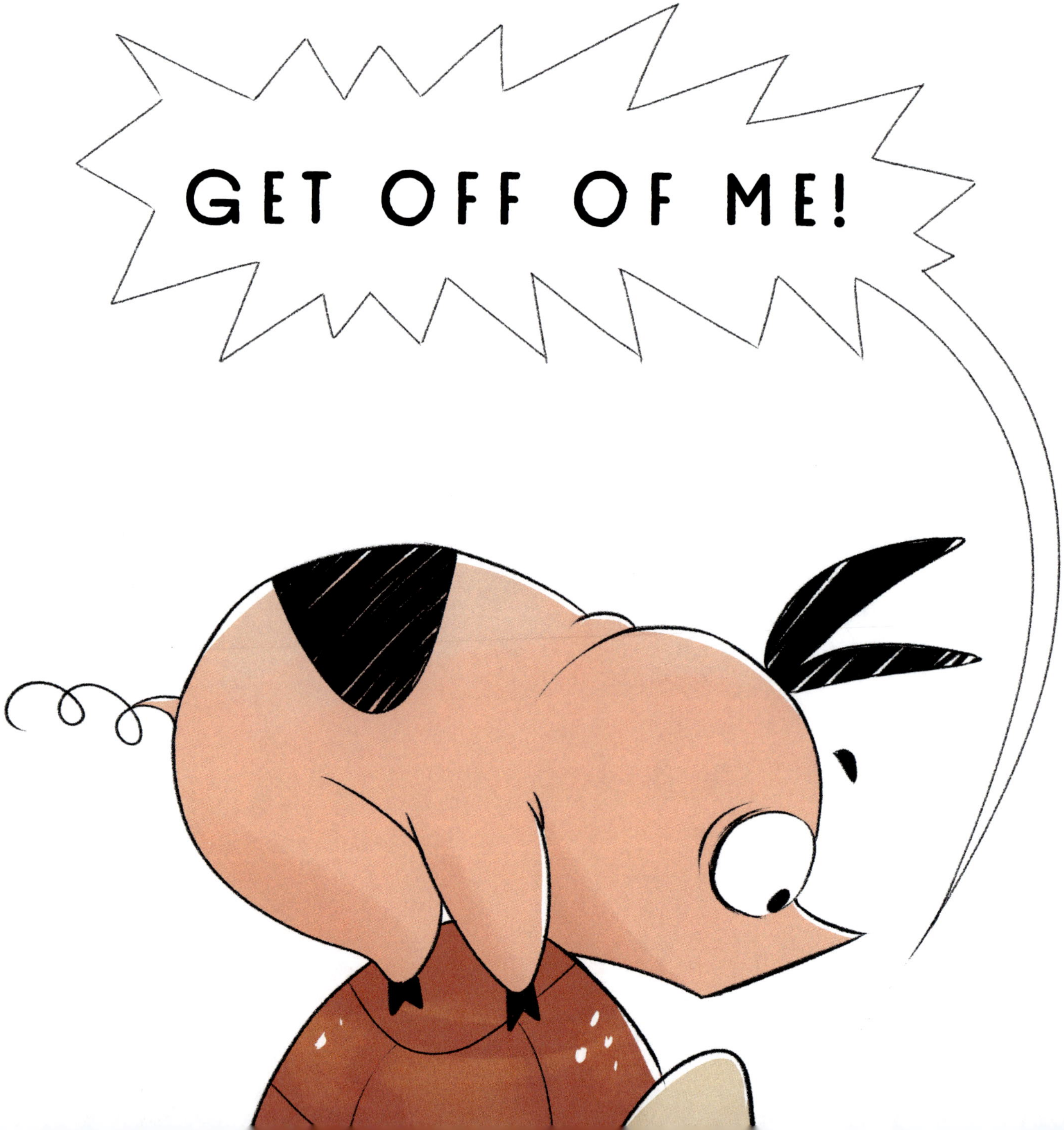
GET OFF OF ME!

Who said that?
Me! Get off me.
Rock?!? Is that you?
A walking **AND** talking rock? Super rare.
I... am a turtle.
Huhhh?

There's no such thing as a walking rock. Or a talking rock. Or a **WALKING, TALKING** rock.

I am just a turtle...

A turtle running away from a hungry piggy.

WAAAIIIIIT!
I'm not trying to eat you!

I've been tracking you all morning so I could give you as a gift to my friend.

She's a rhino. Today's her birthday. But I thought you were a rock.

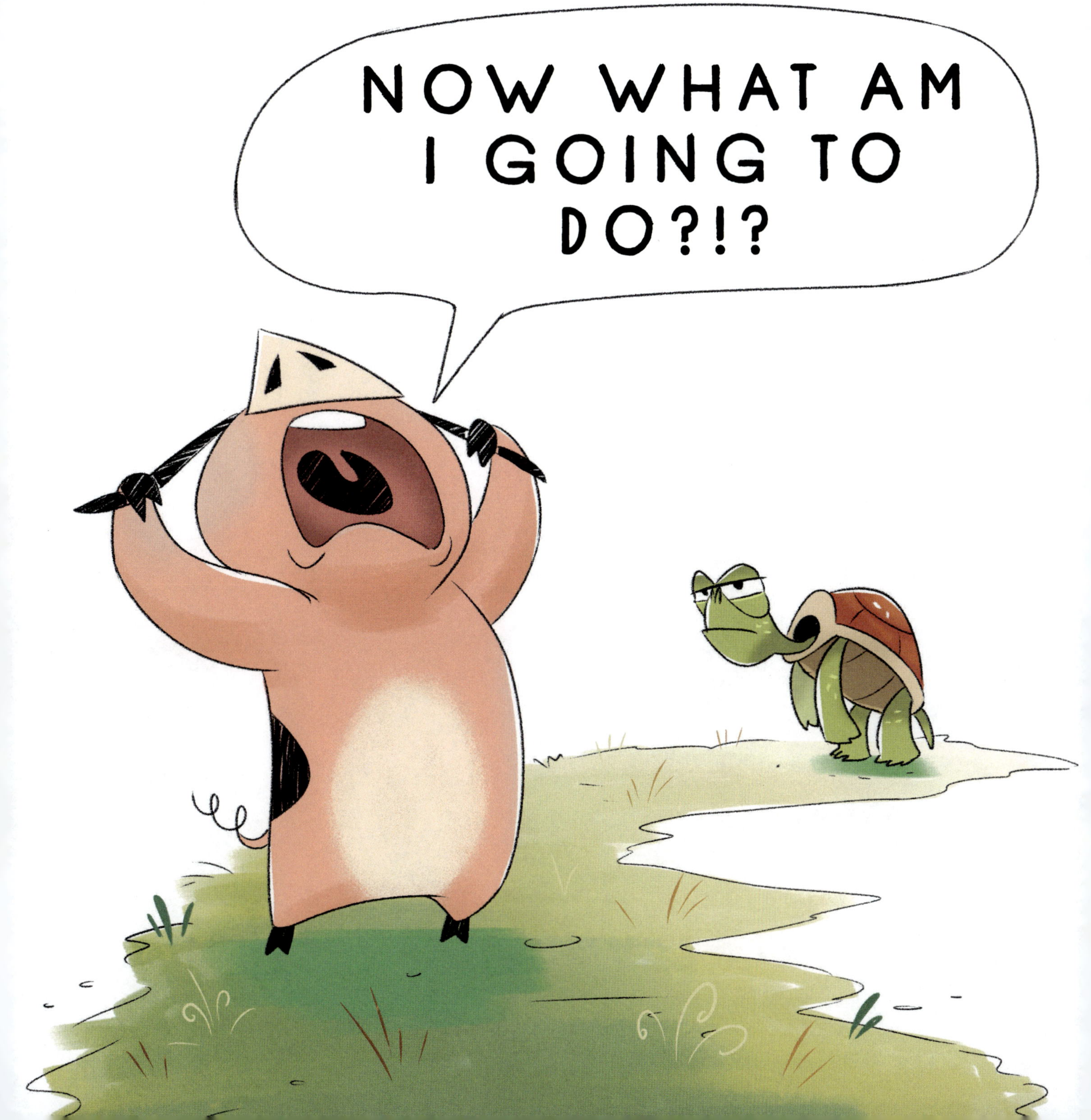
NOW WHAT AM I GOING TO DO?!?

"Your friend's birthday, huh? Don't you think she'd rather spend it with her **FRIENDS** instead of just receive a gift?

A rock gift, no less?"

"Which, by the way - still a turtle."

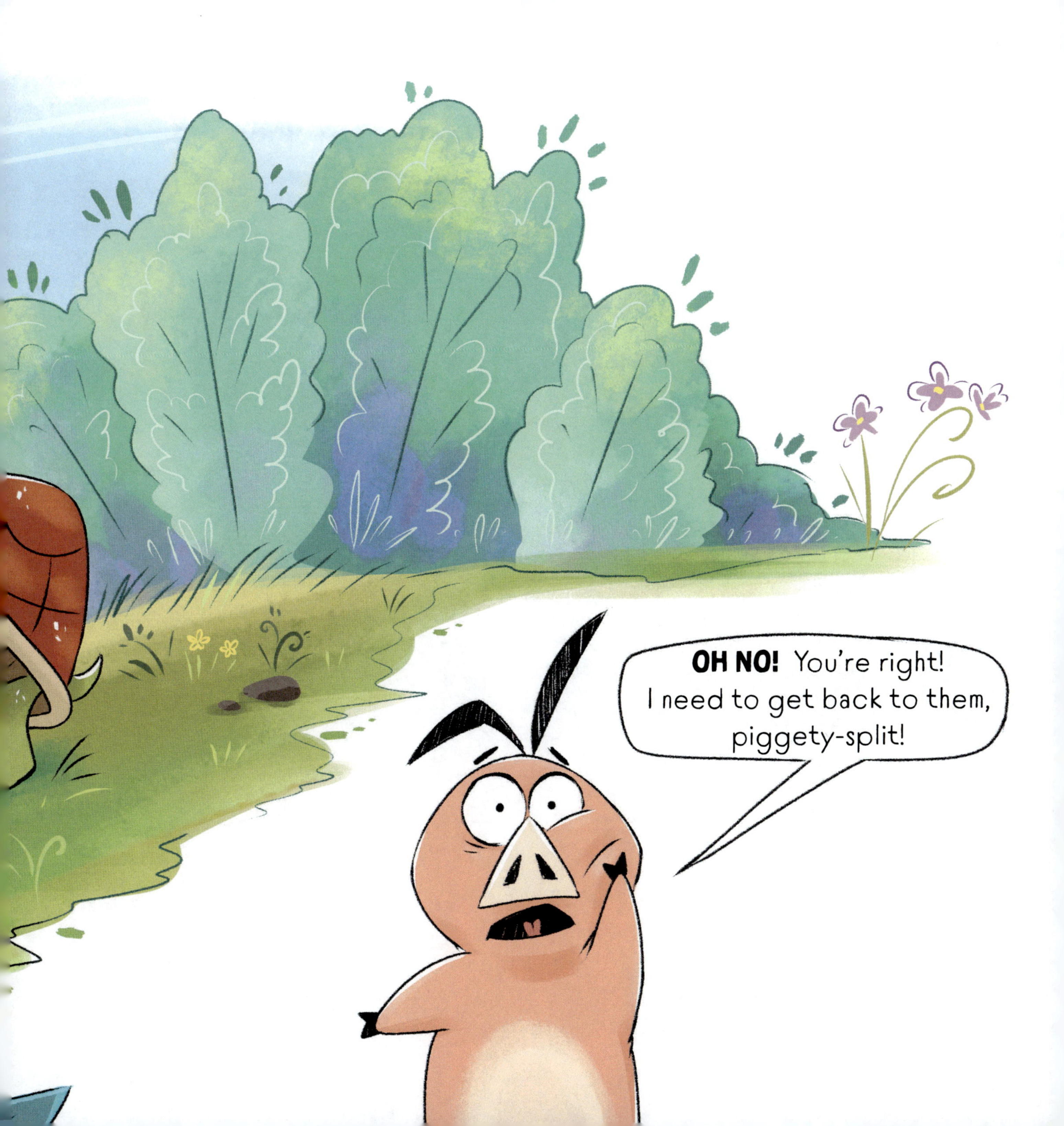
OH NO! You're right! I need to get back to them, piggety-split!

"Well, pig, you're in luck. Turtles are **ACTUAL** expert trackers. If you follow my directions exactly, you will reach your friends... "piggety-split.""

Are you listening?

Yes! Tell me! Tell me!

There. They're right there. Through the leaves. You didn't actually "track" me very far. I'm a turtle, remember?

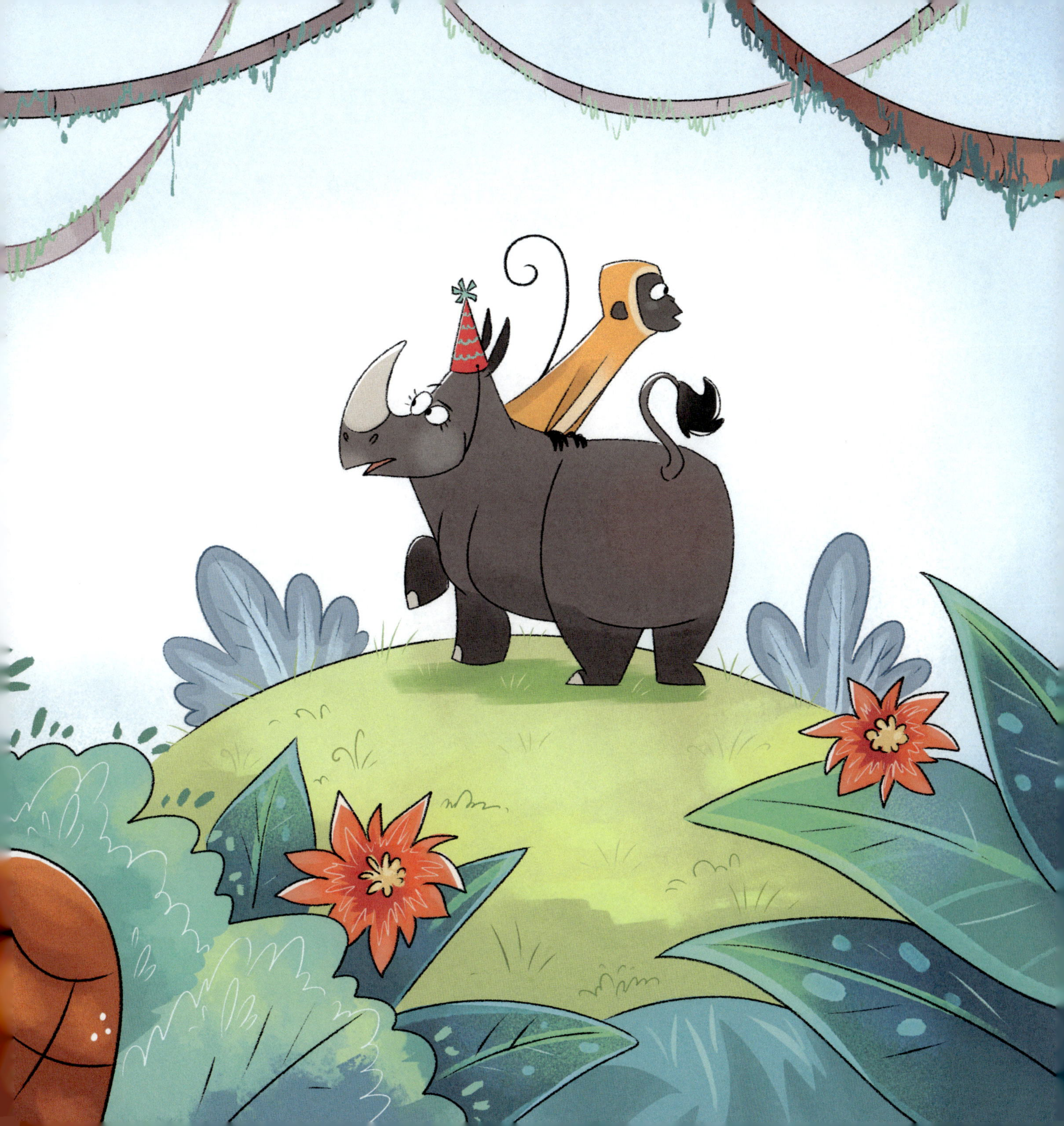

Just then, Hampton's ears perked up, and he heard:

Oink! Oink!   *snort* *snort*   **Piggy! Piggy!**

Overjoyed, he thanked the rock and leapt through the leaves.

Hampton greeted his friends and apologized to each of them... especially Rosie.

"I'm sorry I don't have a gift, Rosie."

"Don't be silly, Hampton. Having my friends with me on my birthday is the best gift I could have wished for!"

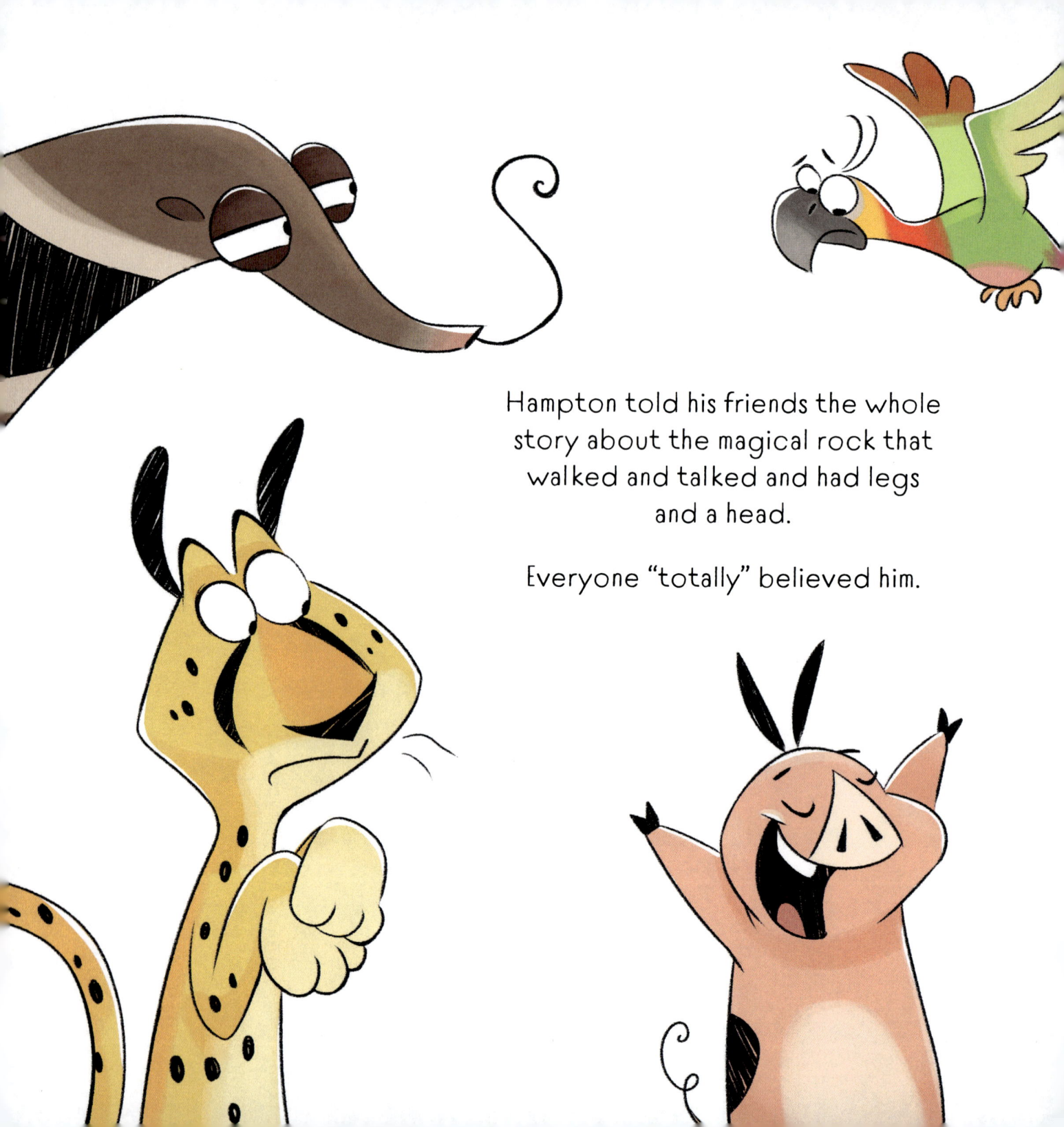

Hampton told his friends the whole story about the magical rock that walked and talked and had legs and a head.

Everyone "totally" believed him.

You were gonna give me a what???

With that, they spent the rest of the day together celebrating Rosie's birthday: eating worms, splashing around, and staying cool.

It turned out to be Rosie's best birthday yet!

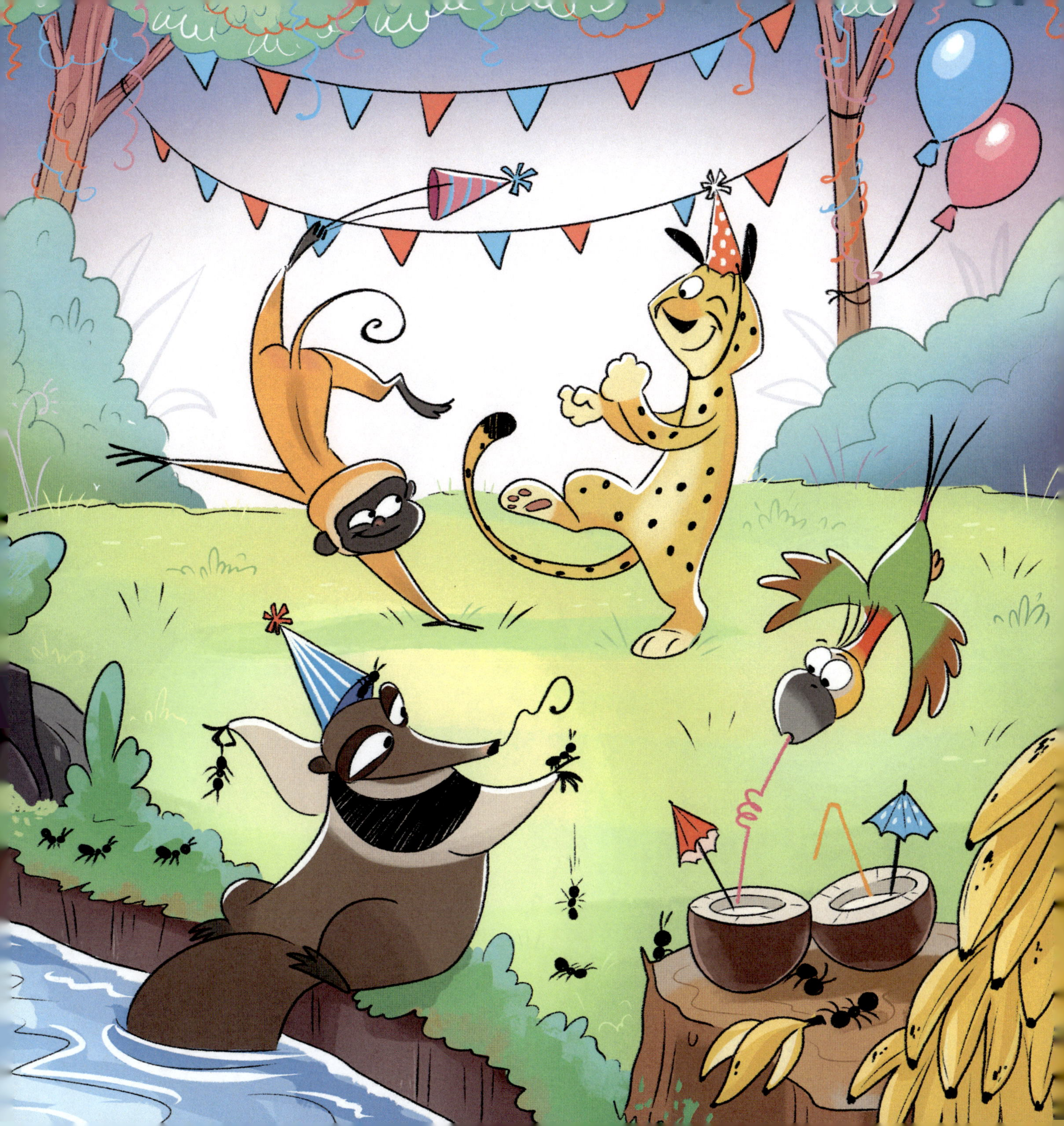

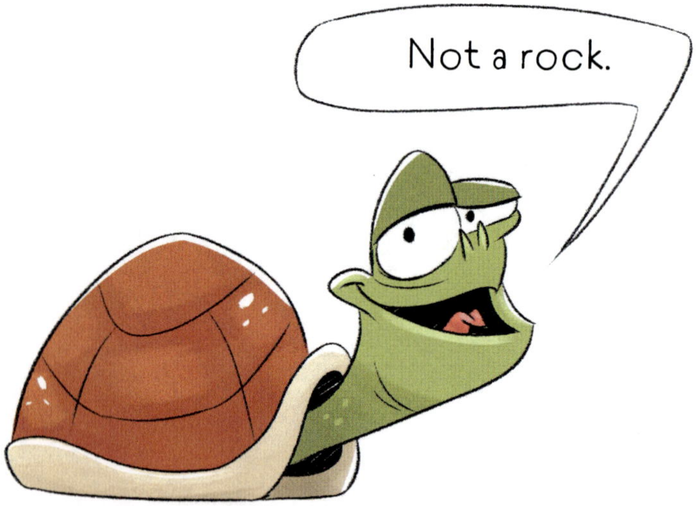
Not a rock.

Made in the USA
Middletown, DE
27 August 2024